The Louisiana Purchase

A Captivating Guide to a Major Turning Point in the History of the United States of America

Free Bonus from Captivating History (Available for a Limited time)

Hi History Lovers!

Now you have a chance to join our exclusive history list so you can get your first history ebook for free as well as discounts and a potential to get more history books for free! Simply visit the link below to join.

Captivatinghistory.com/ebook

Also, make sure to follow us on Facebook, Twitter and Youtube by searching for Captivating History.

Table of Contents

Introduction

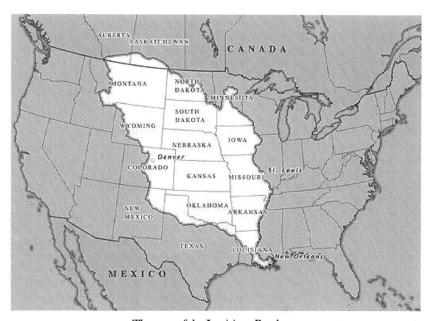

The area of the Louisiana Purchase.

"Every eye in the United States is now fixed on the affairs of Louisiana. Perhaps nothing, since the revolutionary war, has produced more uneasy sensations through the body of the nation."

-Thomas Jefferson, in a letter to Robert R. Livingston on April 18, 1802

The Louisiana Territory encompassed seven entire states, portions of eight additional states, and parts of two Canadian provinces. It was a vast stretch of land bigger than any nation in Western Europe. Stretching from the marshland of the Mississippi Delta to the frozen expanses of North Dakota, the Louisiana Territory was seen by many in the United States and Europe as an almost unending region of untamed wilderness. Of course, almost no one in the US or Europe had ever explored the territory. Thomas Jefferson, who organized the Louisiana Purchase, had never even set foot in New Orleans. Still, he knew that the future of his country rested in securing that port and as much land west of the Mississippi River as possible.

Jefferson, like many in his day, felt that the growing unease in Georgia and Mississippi Territory between Americans and native tribes like the Muscogee (Creek) could be best resolved by relocating Native Americans to new lands. He felt the land west of the Mississippi was perfect for that use. However, to allow Americans to use New Orleans and move Native Americans across the Mississippi, he had to gain control of the Louisiana Territory. This might have meant going to war with Spain or France, neither of which sounded appealing. The United States was a brand-new nation whose military had just defeated the British, but that was a revolutionary war; this would be a war of conquest. Jefferson was not opposed to war but felt he had a better solution.

The Louisiana Purchase was the largest land deal in the history of mankind. However, the borders of the land in question were nebulous at best. The property that France sold the United States was partially claimed by two other European powers and inhabited by thousands of Native Americans formed into hundreds of tribes. Essentially, the sale included Frances' claims west of the Mississippi River, but it did not secure uncontested ownership of the region. So, much of the history of the United States involved establishing that ownership through war, treaty, and exploration. This book will not endeavor to tell that complicated narrative, which is still being played out today. Instead, this book will focus on the forming of the Louisiana Territory, the eventual acquisition of that territory by the United States, and the initial exploration of the territory by representatives of the US. We will also briefly touch on the creation of Indian Territory and tribal reservations within the region and the Louisiana Territory's role in the lead-up to the American Civil War.

It is hard to say precisely what Thomas Jefferson saw on the map when he concluded that it was necessary to make the Louisiana Purchase. Did he see a potential home for the Cherokee, Shawnee, and Muscogee that clashed with American settlers? Did he see the Mississippi River as a great artery bringing goods from the new Ohio Country to the ships in New Orleans and beyond to the great markets of the world? Did he see a commercial empire or a buffer zone for the British in Canada and the Spanish in Texas? Did he see great cities like St. Louis, Denver, and Kansas City far in the future? Whatever he saw, he knew that it was vital for the future of the United States to claim that land, and he was willing to do whatever it took to make it a reality.

Chapter One: Forming the Louisiana Colony

The French came in search of precious metals and a passage to the Pacific Ocean. They would find neither, and perhaps that is part of the reason why the presence of the French in North America seems so ephemeral to us now. After Spain found the "New World" in 1492 and quickly gained riches, other European countries began setting sail to cross the Atlantic. In 1497, John Cabot sailed to Newfoundland for England. Not long after, even Breton and Normand fishermen were catching cod off the coast of what would become Canada. However, it was not until 1523 that François I ordered Giovanni da Verrazano to sail to North America for France. Verrazano, a native of Florence, Italy, was tasked with finding a passage to China. He surveyed the eastern coastline of North America from New Breton Island to the Carolinas. However, Verrazano did not find the famed Northwest Passage to China. Ten years later, Jacques Cartier sailed for North America and got as far as the Gulf of St. Lawrence; there, he met a group of Iroquois Native Americans. On his second voyage, Cartier got as far as the village of Hochelaga, the future site of Montréal. He convinced the French Crown that the nation could benefit from colonizing this new land. However, conflict with Native Americans and between Catholics and Protestants in France stalled the progress of colonization.

In the early 1600s, several expeditions left France for the New World and established trade with Native Americans, primarily in fur. Various colonies were attempted but often abandoned due to conflict with natives. Samuel de Champlain founded Quebec and named the land New France. Various French explorers left Quebec and began to journey through the interior of North America, signing agreements with Native Americans as they went. By the late 1600s, French explorers were traveling throughout the continent despite the misgivings of the French King Louis XIV. They had traveled along the Great Lake region and, by 1672, were now embarking on a survey of the great river that the Native Americans called the "Misi Sipi."

In 1673, René-Robert Cavelier de La Salle set off down the Mississippi River. In 1682, he reached the land of the Quapaw tribe and traveled to the village of Kappa. In what would become Arkansas, La Salle erected a column with the coat of arms of Louis XIV and a painted cross. He claimed the land for France and called it Louisiana after his king. The Quapaw became allied with France. La Salle traveled on and eventually reached the Mississippi Delta in 1682, verifying the belief that the great river flowed into the Gulf of Mexico.

Portrait of René-Robert Cavelier de La Salle.
https://en.wikipedia.org/wiki/File:Cavelier_de_la_salle.jpg

France now claimed a huge crescent of land that stretched from the east coast of Canada to the St. Lawrence River, across the Great Lakes, and down the Mississippi Valley. There were several forts across this expansive empire. The most important fortified town of New France was Quebec, but now it seemed that another fortification was needed at the delta of the Mississippi. With this in mind, La Salle was commanded to take colonists from France to the Mississippi Delta. However, he failed to reach an appropriate spot and instead ran aground on the coast of Texas. There, he was murdered in 1687 by upset colonists who were angry with La Salle's haughty demeanor and poor management of the enterprise—hundreds had died under his command. When word reached Louis XIV of La Salle's expedition, he declared that the land named after him was completely useless. Eventually, however, France realized the importance of La Salle's discovery. By gaining control of the Mississippi, they could limit the spread of their enemy, the English, who were colonizing North America's eastern coastline. Also, this would give them access to a potential trading relationship with Spain, which was close by in Mexico.

In February 1699, an expedition led by a Canadian named Pierre Le Moyne d'Iberville founded the colony of Biloxi in the future state of Mississippi. From there, many expeditions ventured into the new Louisiana Territory. In 1718, Jean Baptiste Le Moyne de Bienville founded another colony among the bays and bayous of the Mississippi Delta. He called the colony La Nouvelle-Orleans, or New Orleans, and this outpost would eventually become the capital of Louisiana Territory in 1723. It was planned out in a grid pattern across what was sometimes called the Isle of Orleans. The buildings were made of wood because little stone could be found in the flood-ridden area.

In 1756, France and Britain waged war on two continents in what would be called the Seven Years' War, or the French and Indian War. Quebec fell to the British in 1759. Seeing one of the anchors of New France fall, France did not want New Orleans to fall to the British, so it looked to an ally. In 1762, after its defeat by the British, France handed Louisiana over to the Spanish.

Nueva Orleans, as the town was then called, became a significant trading center, though Spain was not particularly quick to take control of its new territory. The Spanish king, Charles III, took possession of the territory partly as a consolation for allying with France against Britain and losing but mainly as a buffer to keep the British out of Mexico. At the same time, the French colonists of New Orleans and Louisiana were unhappy about losing their land to a foreign power.

Louisiana was just one part of a Spanish Empire that, at that time, stretched around the globe. Silver production in New Spain had moved from Peru to Mexico by the 1760s, and the Spanish were concerned that foreign interests would try to take the area by force. Because of this, Spain was not interested in colonizing the territory. The transfer from France wasn't formally announced until 1764. The new governor of Louisiana, Don Antonio de Ulloa, did not arrive until 1766, and Spain did not begin to replace French authorities until 1767. Spain did not want to invest money into maintaining a large military presence in Louisiana. The Spanish were outnumbered by not only the Native Americans and Africans but also the French colonists in the area. So, they agreed to allow much of the official business to be conducted not in Spanish but in French. Still, due to the Spanish delay, Ulloa found administrative chaos when he arrived. Ulloa instituted several economic restrictions and ordinances that proved wildly unpopular. Louisiana could only trade with nine ports in Spain; trade with Great Britain and Mexico was banned. Furthermore, the importation of French wine was made illegal. This was a recipe for disaster.

These restrictions quickly caused a rebellion, which Ulloa had no hope of putting down because Spain did not want to send troops to support him. An open revolt in 1768 drove Ulloa out of power. The French colonists petitioned the French government to restore their rule in Louisiana, but it was ignored. The Spanish responded by sending General Alejandro O'Reilly (born Alexander O'Reilly in Ireland) and 2,000 troops to Louisiana. O'Reilly quickly rounded up the rebels and executed twelve men, sentenced others to prison, and confiscated the property of all involved. He abolished the previous Superior Council of Louisiana and instituted the Cabildo, a governing council of ten men overseen by a governor. O'Reilly served as the second governor of Louisiana. He instituted rules that banned the trading of Native American slaves and allowed African slaves to buy their freedom and the freedom of others.

O'Reilly handed over the governorship to Luis de Unzaga y Amézaga in 1769. Unzaga successfully navigated his way between the expectations of the Spanish Crown and the realities of life in Louisiana. He continued O'Reilly's bolstering of providing troops to New Orleans and other outposts along the Mississippi, including St. Louis. He also trained colonists as militias in case the need arose. During times of peace, the soldiers and militia acted as a police force in the territory and were made of white, black, and mixed-race units.

The forts along the Mississippi were nothing more than posts for the fur trade and to continue relations with Native Americans, though there were some settlers as well. A group of French colonists known as the Acadians had been removed from Canada by the British from 1755 to 1764 after the French and Indian War and had made their way to settlements in Louisiana. Many Acadians wanted to leave Louisiana, but Unzaga would not allow it; however, he let them settle in areas within the territory they found more hospitable. Unzaga turned a blind eye to much of the illegal trade with the British in Louisiana because he knew this was the only way to get much-needed supplies to the territory. Still, he regarded the British presence to the east warily.

In 1770, 1,000 British troops reinforced their fort at Pensacola, and Unzaga was concerned that they might try to invade Louisiana. However, this did not come to pass. But six years later, Unzaga saw an opportunity to aid in the revolution of American colonists against Great Britain, so he secretly sold 9,000 pounds of gunpowder to Captain Gibson of the Continental Army without the permission of his king. He sent a message asking for forgiveness, but Carlos III agreed with his decision. Soon, Spain joined France in supporting the American Revolution. However, it did not immediately declare war on the English. Spain had spies in Philadelphia to track the progress of the war against the British. Unzaga retired as governor of Louisiana in 1777 and was succeeded by Bernardo de Gálvez, a career soldier from Málaga, Spain.

Gálvez saw that Spain and Great Britain were the only superpowers in North America and that the British were in the middle of a struggle to retain their control of the thirteen colonies along the Atlantic. It was an excellent opportunity. While the Spanish supported the Americans, they did not want them to win their independence. The Spanish court hoped for a prolonged state of war that would weaken Great Britain's hold in North America but did not want a new, robust nation to be created so close to their interests.

Gálvez did not appear to have the same misgivings. He allowed a representative of the new United States government, a merchant named Oliver Pollock, to use New Orleans as an unofficial depot for troops and supplies to the western theater of the Revolutionary War. Pollock was an Irish-American who spoke fluent Spanish and had lived in New Orleans for many years. He was on good terms with the previous two governors before Gálvez and struck up an immediate friendship with the newest governor.

Then, in June of 1779, Spain declared war on Great Britain, and Gálvez's orders were clear. He was to attack Mobile, Pensacola, and East and West Florida for Spain. However, it was made clear that while France was an ally, the United States was not. This meant that Great Britain was fighting the revolution in the United States and a global war against France and Spain, partly in North America.

When Spain formally declared war, Gálvez knew that the English planned to attack New Orleans and Spanish forts along the Mississippi in Arkansas and Missouri. He had already formed a plan to attack the British before they attacked him. He set out from New Orleans with about 660 men, many of whom were raw recruits and militiamen, just after a devastating hurricane had hit the region. They quickly captured Fort Bute in Manchac, Louisiana, then took the fort at Baton Rouge, followed swiftly by the capture of Fort Panmure. The first was captured by surprise and the second through tenacity, while the third surrendered. All the forts were along the Gulf Coast of what would be the states of Louisiana and Mississippi. They returned to great acclaim, and Gálvez showed himself to be a more than capable general, so he was given that title. Acting Lt. Col. Esteban Miró was made colonel and put in command of the Louisiana Fixed Infantry Regiment. The new treasurer of Louisiana, Martin Navarro, wrote back to Madrid to celebrate the accomplishments of Gálvez and his honorable treatment of his soldiers.

However, the United States was displeased with this turn of events. Many in the Continental Congress were unhappy because, if these forts were in Spanish hands, the Americans could not claim them if they defeated the British. It was clear, even at this embryonic stage, that the people of the United States had clear designs for expanding their territory.

Gálvez was undeterred by or disinterested in the Americans' opinions and planned a campaign to take Mobile and Pensacola in 1780. Under his command were 1,300 soldiers of every rank, file, race, and nation of origin imaginable, including French, Native American, and African. He had several transport ships but only three warships. After setbacks from storms and considerable loss of supplies and ships, he eventually reached Mobile and, after fourteen days of bombardment, took Fort Charlotte. He then moved on to Pensacola, but his force was decimated by a hurricane, and the survivors returned to New Orleans and Havana. In 1781, Gálvez set out again to take Pensacola. This time it would be coordinated from Cuba and he had 8,000 men under his command with assistance from Spanish and French naval forces. In May of 1781, British General John Campbell opened peace negotiations and surrendered all of West Florida to Gálvez.

Finally, in 1783, the war between Great Britain and Spain ended. The next year, the United States secured its independence. The new nation and the old Spanish Empire would need to agree on the border between the US and the Spanish Gulf Coast. Gálvez was made a count and then became viceroy of New Spain but died in 1786 during the typhus epidemic. The new governor of Louisiana was one of Gálvez's commanders, Esteban Rodríguez Miró.

Chapter Two: The Port of New Orleans

In 1788, Charles III, the long-reigning king of Spain, died. That same year, the population of New Orleans reached 5,338 people. The city was composed of French, Spanish, Americans, Native Americans, people of African descent, and combinations of all those. They had developed a new "Cajun" culture that combined the Creole cultures of the Caribbean and the Acadian culture of New France.

The streets were narrow, and the buildings remained much the same as they had been under the French. But on March 21, 1788, Vincente José Núñez, a twenty-seven-year-old army paymaster, retired to an altar in his house and lit between fifty to sixty candles for Good Friday. The combined flames set his ceiling on fire. The fire quickly spread out across the city at an astonishing speed. Of the 1,000 buildings in New Orleans, only 150 remained undamaged, and many were razed. Perhaps because the fire occurred in the middle of the day and the Spanish authorities acted quickly, there was only one fatality. Though more than half the citizens of New Orleans lost their homes within twenty-four hours, no one was without shelter. Many were welcomed into the homes of their neighbors outside the central city. Others received tents from Governor Miró and assistance from the treasurer, Intendant Martín Navarro. Both men handed out biscuits, rice, and small amounts of cash to 700 citizens in need. Miró had flour shipped in from as far away as Philadelphia.

Miró and Navarro, unlike their superiors in Havana and Madrid, were very concerned with the number and prosperity of the citizens of New Orleans and Spanish Louisiana. They were not just concerned with the livelihood of the people in their region. Still, they also believed, especially Intendant Navarro, that Spanish Louisiana could be more than just a buffer zone between the United States and New Spain. Navarro wrote a report deriding the trading regulations imposed on New Orleans, arguing that if this port were opened, fortunes would be made in the trade of indigo, furs, pitch, tar, maize, rice, and slaves.

In fact, in 1783, the Spanish government eased trade restrictions just enough that Navarro had gone from living off his salary of 4,000 pesos to making 24,455 pesos in one year, primarily from selling a cargo of slaves. When the Good Friday fire struck in 1788, Navarro was one of the richest men in New Orleans and loaned 14,000 pesos to one man so he could rebuild after the fire. Even though Spain had not adopted the free trade he wanted in New Orleans, by the time Navarro was fifty, he was worth 3.7 million pesos. He also saw a growing threat to Spain's control of the Mississippi River. After their victory in the Revolutionary War, Americans were crossing the Appalachian Mountains and settling along the Ohio River and its tributaries. As America's footprint grew, it threatened Spanish Louisiana's role as a buffer zone.

The Great New Orleans Fire of 1788 destroyed not only buildings and homes but also records of debts, land ownership, and genealogical records indicating the purity of blood of certain citizens, thus wiping out vital documentation for the territory. After the fire burned out and the homeless were given shelter, it fell upon Governor Miró to begin rebuilding the city. Relief came in many forms from many sources. The French sent supplies and money to the devastated capital, and enterprising merchants ignored Spanish regulations and brought supplies from the United States. One of the most generous benefactors was Don Andrés Almonaster y Roxas de Estrada, whom Miró called a man with a "generous heart." Almonaster had made a fortune in New Orleans through real estate. He served in several official functions and was the commander of the militia at one point. He had built the city's hospital, which was overloaded due to the fire, so he expanded it using his own income. Almonaster would be recognized as the patron who built many of New Orleans' most famous structures, including the St. Louis Cathedral, the new Cabildo building, the Presbytére, and Charity Hospital. The new buildings were made of stone and brick and still stand today.

However, Miró's successor, Francisco Luis Héctor, Baron of Carondelet, discovered that Almonaster was not so magnanimous. Carondelet found Almonaster in possession of regalia of vice royal patronage, something he should not have, so Carondelet took them from Almonaster. Almonaster then stopped his donations to Charity Hospital.

Still, the city was being rebuilt. A new cemetery was built above ground to avoid the continual flooding of the Mississippi. Work was done to build flood walls around the city. Despite the ever-present dangers of hurricanes, floods, and epidemics, New Orleans grew. Perhaps the fastest-growing section of the population was enslaved people. In the 1790s, slaves comprised half the Louisiana Territory's population. It was largely slaves who built flood walls, hospitals, government buildings, and cemeteries. Spanish law prohibited slaves from being brought in from outside markets, but smuggling was rampant, and the authorities chose to look the other way in many cases. Sometimes, this was because they benefitted from the slave trade, and other times, they simply couldn't stop it. After all, it was a problem beyond their control.

Despite stricter building codes after the fire of 1788, another fire broke out in New Orleans in 1794. However, this one was much smaller, burning only 200 structures in the city's southwest corner. The result was that New Orleans became a city of brick buildings. This not only helped in cases of fire but also helped mitigate the effects of the hurricanes that seemed to consistently barrage the Louisiana capital. The city also took on a particularly Spanish feel with pastel colors, courtyards, and detailed wrought iron banisters. The Spanish influences of New Orleans are still apparent today, echoes of the same style seen in Old San Juan in Puerto Rico or Casco Antiguo in Panama City.

The Spanish population increased in New Orleans, and many, like Almonaster, married into French Creole families. This complicated matters when, in 1789, the French Revolution officially began. Spain and France had been allies because of their religious commonality and familial connections. The king of France, Louis XVI, and Spain's monarch, Charles IV, were both from the House of Bourbon. When Louis XVI was deposed and eventually executed, Spain protested, and France declared war on Spain.

This led to increased tensions between Spanish authorities and French settlers in Louisiana. Governor Carondelet quickly deported Frenchmen he considered sympathetic to the revolution. The Spanish, concerned with the situation in Louisiana, knew they needed to increase the population of their territory but could not provide enough Spaniards or other European Catholics. Instead, the Spanish turned to an unlikely source: they began to encourage American immigration to Louisiana.

The logic behind this was complicated. Carondelet wanted to encourage immigration to Spanish Louisiana but wanted immigrants who would become loyal to the Spanish government. He asked Spain to encourage Irish, French, Flemish, and German Catholics to immigrate to Louisiana, but he learned that many of these immigrants were going to the United States instead. He believed these people could be encouraged to travel across the Mississippi to the settlement of New Madrid and reside on the southern Mississippi River. The main thing holding back this immigration, Carondelet believed, was the unfair reputation of Spain's harsh rule.

At the same time, Carondelet was trying to stop the flow of Anglo-American immigrants, who were considered "Goths at the gates of Rome." Carondelet knew the Anglo-Americans in his territory were as likely to turn on their Spanish neighbors as defend them against fellow Americans. They were forced to take loyalty oaths, but the governor knew these were empty promises. Spanish Louisiana needed immigrants who would remain loyal to Spain against all else, including war with France, Britain, or the United States. Carondelet tried various schemes to acquire Catholic European immigrants. For example, a group of French royalists that had unsuccessfully tried to settle in Ohio Country were convinced to travel down the Ohio River to the Mississippi River to settle in Louisiana Territory. However, most of his plans failed. Several agents were sent to Philadelphia to round up immigrants and bring them back to Louisiana, but none were successful.

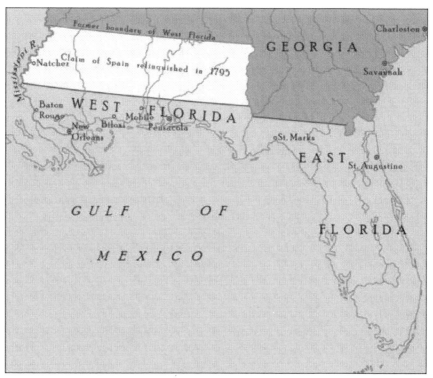

Showing the boundaries established between the United States and Spain in 1795, effective in 1796.

The Treaty of San Lorenzo, or Pinckney's Treaty, in October 1795 established that the 31st parallel from the Mississippi River eastward was the boundary line between the southern United States and the Spanish possessions of Louisiana and Florida. While Spain gave up a considerable amount of land, mainly inhabited by Creek Native Americans, the Crown retained the entire Gulf Coast and so continued to control traffic in the Gulf of Mexico—at least on paper. (Smuggling was still a constant activity that the Spanish vacillated on, ultimately recognizing that they did not have the manpower to stop smuggling operations into and out of Florida and Louisiana.) When the treaty went into effect, global politics shifted again. In 1796, Spain and England were once again at war. Spain, who had been at war with the newly-formed French Republic in the hope of restoring the Bourbon monarchy, had been forced to change positions and formed an alliance with the French Republic against Great Britain.

In Spanish Louisiana, Governor Carondelet was also changing his stance. Concerned that the British would invade Louisiana from Canada, Carondelet agreed to allow Anglo-Americans to immigrate into Louisiana and Florida. This led a man named William Murray to come to New Orleans in 1796 with a proposal to settle 4,000 families of Anglo-Americans in Louisiana. Murray stated that the reason for their immigration was that they were from Kentucky and were dissatisfied with the United States government. In truth, Murray was part of a plot by US General James Wilkinson to separate the western territories of the US from the east and form a new country. Carondelet knew of Murray's involvement in the conspiracy but approved the proposal regardless. His superiors in Spain would not have agreed to such an arrangement.

In 1797, Carondelet's term as governor ended, and his replacement, Manuel Gayoso de Lemos, assumed the position. By then, Anglo-American immigration into Louisiana and Florida had risen sharply. The proverbial genie was out of the bottle. Like Carondelet, Gayoso attempted to stop Anglo-Americans from immigrating into Spanish territory and desperately tried to bring in Spanish colonists (or, at least, European Catholics), but his efforts were too little and too late. When Gayoso died in 1799, Spain simply wanted to be rid of the Louisiana Territory.

It seems to have been unknown to most at the time that US General James Wilkinson, future governor of Louisiana, was a well-paid spy for the Spanish government. At a time when the new US government desperately needed Spain to give them free travel down the Mississippi and the ability to trade in New Orleans, Wilkinson was working with the Spanish government under the codename "Agent 13." He had sworn allegiance to Spain for Governor Miró and had worked for Governor Carondelet, as well. Wilkinson sent the Spanish American secrets he gathered as a brigadier general in the US Army; his messages were always in a cipher. He was almost discovered, but nothing was proven until long after his death. Still, Wilkinson's information was never able to permanently secure Spanish rule in Louisiana, and by 1803, the world had changed again.

Napoleon Bonaparte had risen to be the First Consul of France in 1799. He believed that France needed to expand globally, and part of that included the restoration of New France in North America. Spain, having failed to populate Louisiana with Spanish loyalists and constantly struggling with the United States over navigation rights on the Mississippi, was certainly interested in letting go of the Louisiana Territory. This led to the Third Treaty of San Ildefonso on October 1, 1800. The provisions of this secret treaty were that Spain would give Louisiana back to France. At first, France demanded West and East Florida as well, but Charles IV rejected this proposal. Spain would keep Florida, and in exchange for Louisiana and several warships, Charles IV could place his son-in-law as the Duke of Parma in Italy. Napoleon agreed. He planned to create a French Empire in the New World, anchored by the sugar plantations of Saint-Domingue. Louisiana would provide the raw materials needed to build and maintain the plantations of the Caribbean.

Spain agreed to administer the territory until French officials could arrive, but the process took much longer than expected. Juan Manuel de Salcedo became governor of Louisiana in 1801; he thought he would serve only briefly but stayed in the position for another two years. The United States, now under the leadership of President Thomas Jefferson, got word of the Third Treaty of San Ildefonso in 1801. Jefferson understood that this was a crucial moment in the story of the new republic. The outcome of this exchange could mean great opportunity or war with one or more of the great European empires. He needed to be delicate but also forceful. If France gained Louisiana, it would stop the westward expansion of the United States and could lead to conflict with France, a country he considered a natural ally to the Americans. He decided to act quickly and picked Robert R. Livingston as his emissary.

Livingston was born into a wealthy and influential New York family in 1746. He studied law at King's College (today Columbia University) and helped draft the Declaration of Independence. Livingston was on friendly terms with Jefferson and regularly exchanged letters with George Washington, with whom he shared a great interest in agriculture. Robert Livingston and his brother were also keenly interested in steam power and helped finance Robert Fulton's revolutionary steamship *Clermont*, named after Livingston's estate. Jefferson named him minister plenipotentiary to France, a position Jefferson himself had held. Livingston was to approach the French with an offer to purchase the Louisiana Territory.

However, there were considerable difficulties with Livingston's mission. Mainly, it was not clear that Jefferson's actions were constitutional. There were indeed a large number of leaders in the United States who would argue that Livingston's mission was completely illegal and illogical. Jefferson and Livingston were among the so-called

Anti-Federalists. The opposition, the Federalists, were not convinced that the United States should be spreading west at all. They believed that America did not need the Louisiana Territory and certainly could not afford to buy it from France. They were not convinced that having Spain or France as western neighbors was of any concern to the people in the eastern United States. The land of Louisiana was, they felt, a great wilderness teeming with hostile Native Americans and dangerous animals. There was not a clear use for this land.

Jefferson disregarded these criticisms and sent Livingston to determine if Spain had given Louisiana and Florida to France and, if so, what Napoleon's intentions might be. Livingston had to deal with the famous French foreign minister Charles Maurice de Talleyrand, known for his intelligence and skill in politics. Livingston got directly to the point, asking if Spain was giving Louisiana and Florida to France and if France intended to pay off her debt with the land. Talleyrand replied that only fools paid off debts with land, but the land was not France's to use regardless. He denied the existence of the Third Treaty of San Ildefonso.

Then Livingston began speaking with Joseph Bonaparte, the First Consul's older brother. He offered Joseph Bonaparte a scheme in which France could give Louisiana and Florida to the United States. Then, upon the death of Napoleon, the US could provide land directly to the Bonaparte family. It was a somewhat outlandish plan, but it appealed to Joseph's concerns for the family after his brother's eventual death. Once Talleyrand heard of these conversations, Livingston was told he could no longer speak to Joseph on these matters and must speak only with Talleyrand. Livingston said that the US would go as far as to ally with Great Britain to keep Louisiana open.

In October of 1802, the intendant of Louisiana, Juan Ventura Morales, closed the port of New Orleans to all American traffic. Morales held the same position as Martín Navarro and, like Navarro, had become very rich, though he was generally unliked by the governors he had worked with. Governor Manuel Juan de Salcedo pointed out that Morales had violated Pinckney's Treaty of 1795. Morales, however, claimed that he had studied the treaty's details and found that the Americans' right of deposit in New Orleans had lapsed and could only be renewed by an order directly from the king. This meant that no American could ship cargo to New Orleans and sell it in the market there. The previous year, the United States had accounted for well over a million dollars' worth of sales in the port of New Orleans. When word reached Kentucky and Ohio, farmers and merchants were in an uproar.

It took five weeks for the news to reach Washington, but once Jefferson heard of it, he was convinced it was the lone act of an overzealous bureaucrat, namely Morales. The Spanish ambassador assured Secretary of State James Madison that Morales had acted independently. The western citizens of the US were not easily convinced and believed that Morales had acted under orders from the king—who was, in turn, working in concert with Napoleon. Papers in Kentucky began to report that a French army had taken New Orleans or, at least, that one was on its way. Many in the west were calling for war, and others in the northeast were echoing their calls, if only because they despised France. Jefferson only hoped the situation would resolve itself before long.

In truth, Morales had not been acting on his own but had received a secret order from Charles IV to shut down New Orleans to the Americans because he believed the Americans were taking advantage of their right of deposit and involved in a good amount of smuggling. This might have been accurate, but Charles IV did not want to be seen as giving the order, so Morales blamed himself. The order had been so well covered up that it would take decades to discover the truth. Regardless, when Napoleon heard the news of Morales' actions, he was delighted. Part of his plan for a New World empire involved removing the Americans from New Orleans and the Mississippi so that they could be used exclusively by the French. His happiness was short-lived, however, because not long after news of the New Orleans port crisis reached France, more devastating news followed. In the wake of this new information, Napoleon's plan, and thus the fate of the world, would completely change.

Chapter Three: Purchasing a Colony

Napoleon's sister, Pauline, was known as something of a strumpet and could be quite crass about her relations. She claimed to have even slept with her famous brother. Napoleon was, therefore, instrumental in encouraging her marriage to Colonel Charles Victor Emmanuel Leclerc in 1801. Along with the union, Leclerc was made a general and given a particularly important assignment.

Depiction of General Charles Leclerc.
https://commons.wikimedia.org/wiki/File:Leclerc,_g%C3%A9n%C3%A9ral_en_chef...arm%C3%A9e_de_Saint-Domingue.jpg

Leclerc was to travel to the French colony of Saint-Domingue and restore order. Saint-Domingue existed on a portion of the island of Hispaniola that is today called Haiti. It was the site of one of the cruelest colonies in the Americas but also the birthplace of a powerful movement toward freedom. The importance of Leclerc's role in the colony and the colony's role in Napoleon's plans could not be overstated. The outcome of Leclerc's mission would forever shape the future of the Louisiana Territory and, by extension, all of the United States. Farmers in Ohio, enraged by the closure of New Orleans, could not have imagined that the invasion of an island 1,600 miles away would play such a crucial role in their prosperity, but such was the beginning of globalism.

In the 18th century, Saint-Domingue had become France's wealthiest colony due to large sugar, indigo, coffee, and cotton plantations worked by a vast army of slave labor. When the French Revolution broke out in 1789, the colony was deeply divided. The wealthy plantation owners wanted to break ties with France, while the enslaved population, inspired by the rhetoric of the French Revolution, desired freedom for themselves. There were about 40,000 whites in the colony—some of them plantation owners, some of them craftsmen. Some owned hundreds of slaves, and some owned only a few. Of those of African descent in the colony, 30,000 were free, an unknown number had escaped, and 500,000 remained enslaved.

The Haitian Revolution, the largest and most successful slave rebellion in the Western Hemisphere, began in 1791. Slaves outnumbered whites 10 to 1 and were led by former slave Toussaint L'Ouverture (Louverture), a charismatic and brilliant fighter. In all, some 100,000 rebels died, as did 24,000 whites. L'Ouverture's forces beat off both French reinforcements and a British army in 1793. By 1801, L'Ouverture had taken the Spanish colony of Santo Domingo, abolished slavery on the island, and declared himself governor-general for life.

Napoleon had tasked his brother-in-law to retake the island. Though he did not come right out and say it, it seems plausible to conclude that Leclerc was to reinstitute slavery and bring Saint-Domingue back as the richest of France's colonies. Leclerc was to have somewhere around 40,000 troops to accomplish this, with more following behind him. Once Saint-Domingue had been reclaimed, the French were to go to New Orleans and take possession of Louisiana, removing any American forces that might try to stop them. When Leclerc's ships arrived, L'Ouverture was impressed with the French forces but used guerilla tactics to harass them as they tried to take the island. Leclerc quickly took many key portions of the island. He perhaps hoped his work was done when he captured L'Ouverture and sent him as a prisoner to France, where he died.

However, one of L'Ouverture's generals, another former slave named Jean-Jacques Dessalines, took control of the rebel army, which was now convinced the French had come to reinstitute slavery. They defeated the French at the Battle of Vertières on November 18, 1803. By that time, Charles Leclerc was already dead from yellow fever. Of his original troops, less than half survived the campaign. Leclerc's successor, General Rochambeau, was needlessly cruel, torturing prisoners and conducting mass drownings. This only made the rebels angrier and convinced them to fight harder. Dessalines drove the French from the colony and renamed the country Haiti. France would be the first to recognize the new nation. It was the second colony, after the United States, to gain its freedom from a European power.

When news of the failure to retake Saint-Domingue reached Napoleon, he erupted in anger. "Damn sugar, damn coffee, damn colonies!" he yelled at a dinner party in January 1803. Napoleon now had to rethink his whole strategy. Saint-Domingue was the key to forming an empire in the New World, and without it, Louisiana suddenly lost all its importance. Additionally, many of the ships that were supposed to carry soldiers to Saint-Domingue and then Louisiana were being blockaded in their French ports by the British. The French and British had previously signed the Treaty of Amiens in March 1802 and temporarily gained peace. However, Napoleon realized that with the failure of his West Indies expedition, war with the English was inevitable. To facilitate such a direct conflict, he needed funds.

In secrecy, Napoleon told his brothers, Minister Talleyrand, and Director of the Treasury François Barbé-Marbois that he believed he would sell Louisiana. The Bonaparte brothers and Talleyrand were opposed, but Barbé-Marbois saw the benefit. Napoleon declared that he would tolerate no opposition. To him, it was better to sell the colony for a profit than eventually lose it to the British, who could invade Louisiana from Canada. In confidence, Napoleon told Barbé-Marbois, "I renounce Louisiana...I renounce it with the greatest regret. To attempt obstinately to retain it would be folly." He instructed the treasurer to sell it for fifty million francs. Napoleon knew that the land would make America powerful in the centuries to come, but he needed to face the threat at hand.

James Monroe was made a consul to France at the beginning of 1803 and was on his way to Paris when Napoleon instructed Barbé-Marbois to make a deal with Robert Livingston. The crisis of the Mississippi was boiling over in the United States, and Congress was settling on how to proceed with a conquest of the Louisiana Territory. News of the escalation of cries for war in the United States reached Paris roughly the same time Monroe arrived. Perhaps it was this that made Talleyrand change his opinion and favor the sale of Louisiana.

Livingston met with Talleyrand, but the French minister continued to act as though France did not have possession of Louisiana. Livingston replied that then the US was likely to take it by force from Spain. Talleyrand grew alarmed and wondered aloud if the US would be interested in the whole colony, not just New Orleans. Livingston stated that he was instructed to purchase New Orleans and the Floridas, but Talleyrand countered that without New Orleans, the rest of Louisiana was worthless. Talleyrand asked what the US would give for the whole colony, ignoring the question of the Floridas. Livingston said they might buy it for twenty million francs, but Talleyrand said that was too low. Livingston suggested they wait for the arrival of Monroe.

In early April 1803, Barbé-Marbois called on Livingston. In a quiet conversation, they approached the subject of purchasing Louisiana. Barbé-Marbois suggested an amount of 100 million francs. Livingston said it was too high but vaguely offered sixty million francs for the colony. Once Monroe arrived, the Americans settled on a limit of fifty million francs, but their first offer would be forty million. After a series of meetings between Livingston, Monroe, Talleyrand, and Barbé-Marbois, they settled on a price, the same that Livingston had offered to Barbé-Marbois: sixty million francs plus twenty million francs of French debt owed to US citizens, amounting to roughly $15 million.

Because Napoleon wanted his money as quickly as possible, the US financed the purchase through bonds sold to two banking houses, Hope & Co. out of Amsterdam and the John & Francis Baring & Company based out of London. The British government allowed this transaction to take place because it was preferable to have Louisiana in US hands than French. However, once war broke out between England and France in December 1803, John & Francis Baring & Company was instructed to no longer make payments to the French government.

One stipulation of the purchase was that Louisiana's citizens be incorporated into the United States as quickly as possible and given the same rights and freedoms that US citizens enjoyed. Neither Monroe nor Livingston took issue with that, and they signed the agreement on April 30, 1803. The purchase would still need to be ratified by the United States government, and there was some question about this. It was not clear that the Constitution gave the president the right to make such a land purchase on behalf of the country. Jefferson and his allies must find some way to allow the purchase, or Louisiana might fall through their hands. The citizens of Louisiana were certainly unsure about their prospects, as were the traders trying to move cargo down the Mississippi.

In Paris, copies of the agreement were finalized in both English and French. Napoleon summoned Monroe and Livingston and told them that, with the Louisiana Purchase, he had created a rival for Great Britain. Livingston recognized the momentous treaty. "From this day," he wrote, "the United States take their place among the powers of the first rank."

It was not until June 1803 that news of the purchase reached the United States. Jefferson and his supporters were ecstatic. Many in the US celebrated. Not only had war been averted, but America had just doubled in size. Americans, ever hungry for land and opportunity, saw promise in the unknown expanses of Louisiana. However, the treaty was vague about the actual borders of Louisiana. Jefferson calculated that he had just purchased roughly 500 million acres, which was very close to the mark. The official treaty arrived in Washington on July 14, 1803, along with letters from both Monroe and Livingston. The two delegates were apologetic in their tone. They had been instructed to buy New Orleans but had come away with the entire colony, a huge swath of the continent.

Jefferson called together his Cabinet to discuss the purchase. First, they recognized that Livingston and Monroe had exceeded expectations. Jefferson believed this would end the embargo of New Orleans. He sent word to the governor of Mississippi Territory and the head of the western army to prepare to take possession of the city and allow Americans to deposit their cargo as they wished. Jefferson had to acknowledge the fact that Livingston and Monroe had also been instructed to purchase the Floridas as well, but it was revealed that this was not under French ownership. Everyone agreed that it was of little importance. The treaty would need to be ratified by both the Senate and Congress. Jefferson had the votes in the Senate to pass it without issue, but he was not so certain about Congress. The Senate would be called on October 17, so Jefferson had time to prepare his arguments.

One of Jefferson's chief concerns was that his purchase of Louisiana was not a power of the executive branch spelled out in the Constitution. He knew his opponents, primarily the Federalists, would not allow such a bold move by the president without a fight. Jefferson, not so long before, had argued against such actions by the president. He was a proponent of small government, and buying 500 million acres of land with $15 million from the US Treasury was not an example of a small government.

Jefferson was also concerned about the Native Americans—not the Native Americans living in Louisiana Territory but those living within Mississippi Territory and the Ohio Country. When he was younger, he believed America needed to treat Native Americans justly above all else. But now that he was in the White House, it seemed that his primary concern should be for US citizens, which did not include Native Americans. He saw a possible solution in this new purchase. The Native Americans living in Mississippi, Tennessee, Georgia, and the Carolinas could be offered land west of the Mississippi in Louisiana Territory. They could be moved there and live as they saw fit if they didn't want to adopt the white culture and live as Americans did. This idea would lead from Jefferson to another president, Andrew Jackson, and the Indian Removal Act that created the Trail of Tears.

Though Jefferson faced obstacles to the finalization of the Louisiana Purchase, he was confident they would be overcome. There was a brief flurry of concern that Napoleon was planning to back out of the deal, but he was mollified by Monroe, who saved the purchase with a quick infusion of another two million dollars. Though both men would claim credit years later, it was truly the partnership of Livingston and Monroe that secured the Louisiana Purchase.

Jefferson, always a multitasker, had other plans, as well. As early as 1802, he had begun planning a scientific expedition into Louisiana Territory, and he believed his personal secretary at the time would be the best man to lead it. His name was Meriwether Lewis, and he was twenty-eight years old.

Lewis, born in Charlottesville, Virginia, in 1774, had been inquisitive and adventurous from a young age. His father had died when he was a child, and his mother remarried. The family moved to Georgia. At age thirteen, he returned to Virginia to receive a formal education and learn how to run the family plantation. He then enlisted in the army and served under Washington in the Whiskey Rebellion. He later served in the elite Chosen Rifle Company, then under the command of a young man named William Clark. Lewis was a capable soldier and eventually rose to the rank of captain. It was then he came to be employed by President Jefferson.

Jefferson liked the young man immensely. "His courage was undaunted," the president once explained. "His firmness and perseverance yielded to nothing but impossibilities; a rigid disciplinarian, yet tender as a father to those committed to his charge; honest, disinterested, liberal, with a sound understanding and a scrupulous fidelity to truth."

The president soon had Lewis learning from the greatest botanists, physicians, and scientists of the age. The goal of the mission, Jefferson concluded, would be to not only explore the Louisiana Purchase but find a water route to the Pacific Ocean—something that had been dreamed of for centuries. Lewis was to keep track of everything they encountered and chart their passage as they went. Louisiana Territory was then a vast area of unknowns, and Lewis' expedition would strive to give shape to uncharted territory.

Yet, the treaty was still not ratified. After months of deliberating on how to handle the constitutional questions of the purchase, Jefferson was still uncertain about the best approach. At first, he believed he needed a constitutional amendment to allow him to make the deal, but Secretary Madison thought that was unnecessary. Finally, he decided the best approach was no approach at all. The supporters of the treaty would not bring up the constitutional question. On October 20, 1803, the Senate met and ratified the treaty with a vote of twenty-four for and seven against. All those who voted against it were Federalists.

Though the treaty had been ratified, the nation was not in the clear. In reaction to the Louisiana Purchase, a group of Federalists in New England was brewing a new conspiracy that threatened to tear the nation apart. The actions of these northern politicians would be echoed by Southerners many years later. It was believed that with the Louisiana Purchase, the southern states would become too powerful and dominate the northern states. The solution, many northerners concluded, was simple: secede from the Union.

Chapter Four: Opposition and Preparation

On October 27, 1803, the United States Congress met to debate "An act to enable the President of the United States to take possession of the territories ceded to the United States by France...and for a temporary government thereof." Congress had been debating the entire Louisiana issue since the previous year. In February 1803, several months before the purchase, Jefferson had already secured $2,500 from Congress for external commerce, which would fund the Lewis and Clark Expedition. Now, in October, Congress debated how the new territory was to be administrated. Were the people currently living in Louisiana to be given full citizenship, or were they more like colonists or subjects with no representation in the government? Who would govern this territory, which was as large as the current United States? Would a governor be appointed? Who would the governor answer to?

Many in Congress were hesitant to give the executive branch too much power. They desired the president to have administrative power for only a short time. Debates continued into the next day, but eventually, the motion was passed with amendments limiting the president's powers in a vote of eighty-nine for and twenty-three against. Jefferson was to provide a governor for the territory and military and judicial bodies to ensure the peaceful transition of power. Jefferson sent Mississippi governor William C.C. Claiborne to be the new territorial governor of Louisiana, and to assist him was General James Wilkinson.

They were to go immediately to New Orleans and present themselves. Proper procedures demanded that, first, Spain would have to officially hand over Louisiana to France; then, France would need to hand over Louisiana to the United States. There was a slight difficulty in that the people of New Orleans were not yet aware their colony had been sold. This happened to include the new French governor.

Pierre Clément de Laussat had been born into a family of government officials. Red tape, one might say, was in his blood. He had been tossed around during the French Revolution but had come through in one piece. When Napoleon gained Louisiana back from Spain, Laussat asked for the position of colonial prefect. When Laussat and his family set sail from France, Louisiana was still very much a French colony. But, by the time they arrived in New Orleans, it had been sold to the United States. From March until August 1803, Laussat began planning for what he assumed would be a long and fruitful career running this vast colony. Then news arrived that Laussat's tenure would be short-lived: he was to hand over Louisiana in December.

On November 30, 1803, Juan Manuel Salcedo, the Spanish governor, handed over the keys to New Orleans's fortification to Laussat and announced that all the citizens of Louisiana were released from their oath of fealty to the Spanish Crown. Three weeks later, Laussat handed those same keys to Claiborne in a civil ceremony in the Cabildo. The territory of Louisiana was now in the United States' hands without difficulties or bloodshed. Laussat would go on to serve as the colonial prefect in Martinique, where he was captured by the British. After being released, he was governor of French Guiana until 1823. In recognition of his service to his country, he was made a baron. He died in France in 1835.

The new governor's primary concern was the presence of two large companies of black militiamen that had been part of the Spanish defenses of Louisiana. Claiborne did not need to be told that many in the US, especially in the South, would have difficulty accepting well-armed people of color within their borders. The fear, for these people and Claiborne, stemmed from the recent events in Saint-Domingue and the revolt that had pushed the French off the island. The free people of color might vary easily conspire with the slave population. This combined force—which would most likely be greater than the white population—could seek to take the territory for themselves. Claiborne's difficulty lay in the fact that if he decommissioned the two militia companies, he would offend those men and push them into revolt. However, if he left the companies as they were, there would be considerable backlash from the rest of the nation. The governor consulted Jefferson, who told him to leave the companies as they were until the situation presented a better solution.

It was not just the black militia that concerned the rest of America. Louisiana consisted of a three-caste system within the common population. The Europeans served mainly as officials and military leaders. The vast majority of the population could be split into three groups: French-speaking Creoles, free people of color, and enslaved persons. This did not easily translate into the black and white dichotomy of the United States. The presence of elites with multiethnic backgrounds was problematic to Claiborne and the Americans that followed him. One of Claiborne's first acts was to send out a proclamation concerning the transition of Louisiana to the United States. In it, he promised equal citizenship but did not specify who exactly would receive this citizenship or when. The proclamation, for reasons of practicality, had to be printed in three languages: English, French, and Spanish. This was something very radical to a country that had remained fairly homogeneous and recognized one language, for the most part. The process of bringing Louisiana officially into the US would take years.

Yet, there were those in the US who were not as concerned with the diversity of Louisiana as they were with the potential for it to unbalance the power of their country. Some felt it was a waste of money on land that wasn't needed. They envisioned a vast wilderness home to only wolves and Native Americans. Others saw it as an expansion of the South, under the control of Virginia, into an empire that would be turned into slave states, giving the South the ability to overpower the North. Thanks to the Three-Fifths Clause of the Constitution, any person who wasn't free was considered three-fifths of a person when determining congressional representation. If Louisiana was flooded with slaveholders and slaves, Congress would be forever controlled by slaveholders and the interests of the South. Since these interests were often at odds with the North, many Northerners viewed Louisiana as a death knell to their way of life.

Chief among these was a senator from Essex County in Massachusetts named Timothy Pickering. The senator envisioned the northern states breaking away from the Union and, perhaps along with some Canadian provinces, forming a "Northern Confederacy." Pickering had supporters and even toyed with the idea of Aaron Burr, from New York, leading the secession. But Burr lost his bid for governor of New York and then killed Alexander Hamilton in a duel, which caused him to lose a good deal of political clout. Pickering couldn't get enough support for his movement and eventually shelved it. However, his arguments would be echoed decades later—in the mouths of southern politicians.

Part of the problem with getting Americans to completely oppose the Louisiana Purchase was the fact that Americans, as a rule, simply love a good deal. At four cents an acre, the Louisiana Purchase was, as French Minister Talleyrand put it, "a noble bargain." Part of the fear that Americans felt about the territory was also part of the allure. It was almost entirely uncharted, and the borders would not be settled until at least 1819. Americans knew it was vast and dangerous but also full of potential. There were rivers and fast streams perfect for milling operations. There was the potential for mining copper, tin, lead, and perhaps even gold. There were countless miles of untamed forests from which limitless timber could be procured. From the few existing descriptions, the land was said to be amazingly fertile. Beyond the lowlands near the Mississippi, it was said, was rich and dark soil that would grow anything planted in it. Eli Whitney's cotton gin had been patented in 1794, and the growth of "King Cotton" was making Louisiana look like a veritable promised land to those wanting to establish cotton plantations.

Jefferson knew that, to make the most out of his new territory, he needed a survey conducted and that the rivers especially needed to be mapped. Also, he desired a general scientific exploration of the types of animals, plants, and people to be found there. He envisioned a relatively small group of fully-provisioned men entering Louisiana Territory, traveling the width of the continent to the Pacific Ocean, and then returning. Later historians would compare it, reasonably, to NASA's moon landing in 1969. Although this group would be part of the US Army, it was not a military force. They were not meant to conquer or subdue any Native American nations or defend anyone besides themselves if attacked. They were essentially scouts, providing Jefferson and the rest of the country with vital information about their new acquisition. As stated, Jefferson had acquired $2,500 for the expedition and had chosen Meriwether Lewis to command it. While the rest was ostensibly up to Lewis, Jefferson provided insight and help where needed.

Lewis' instructions from the President seemed straightforward enough. He was to follow the Missouri River, which fed into Mississippi near the settlement of St. Louis, to determine a direct route to the Pacific. Jefferson hoped there might be a water route to the western ocean— the supposed Northwest Passage. Lewis was to fix the longitude and latitude at any important points on the journey and take copious notes and observations that would be interesting to himself and anyone else who would read them. Jefferson wanted detailed accounts of all the people that Lewis met—their general number, possessions, traditions, and languages. Lewis was to note the soil, vegetation, and animals he encountered, especially animals that might have been deemed rare or extinct. Jefferson even thought there might be a chance that Lewis would encounter living mammoths on his expedition. Jefferson told Lewis to keep several copies of his journal and have them carried by different people in the party to avoid loss and damage.

Portrait of Meriwether Lewis by Charles Wilson Peale.
https://commons.wikimedia.org/wiki/File:Meriwether_Lewis-Charles_Willson_Peale.jpg

The year 1803 was largely spent in preparation for the expedition. Lewis at first believed he could cross the Appalachian Mountains by summer, go to Tennessee to find recruits, and arrive in St. Louis by August. He hoped to then travel up the Missouri River until he was forced to camp for winter. Then he would cross the "Stony Mountains," travel to the Pacific Ocean, and return before the winter of 1804. This would turn out to be a great underestimation. A British expedition had crossed these mountains (now called the Rocky Mountains) in the snowy north, and many believed them to be no more than 3,000 feet in elevation. It was generally believed that no mountains in North America exceeded the height of the Blue Ridge Mountains or the Appalachians. That, however, was not what kept Lewis from reaching St. Louis much later than August.

Captain Lewis went to Harper's Ferry and purchased fifteen flintlocks, muzzle-loading .54 caliber rifles, plus a dozen pipe tomahawks. These were just the beginning. While the Lewis and Clark Expedition ran out of many supplies, they were never short of rifles or shots. This was by design. Lewis knew that a good rifle and a sharp knife were among the key necessities for traveling in the wilderness. He had worked as a paymaster in the Ohio Country and traveled constantly, often by himself, through the dense wilderness. There were no roads to speak of, only a few Native American paths and waterways. He knew how to navigate. From his mother, he had learned the medicinal qualities of wild plants, and he knew how to hunt and dress game. His time in the army had taught him discipline, and his time as Jefferson's secretary had made him an intimate friend of the president who knew his wishes and designs. Jefferson's library, perhaps the best on the continent, was open to Lewis.

Jefferson had also sent him to be trained in a wide variety of subjects. From Dr. Benjamin Rush, Lewis learned the basics of medicine and field surgery. He knew how to set a broken bone and treat a fever. He purchased the newest technology in navigation and could determine his longitude and latitude in the middle of a forest. He learned cartography, geology, and a wide array of botany. He could identify plants, give them their Latin names, and list their uses.

Lewis and Jefferson had spent countless hours determining the best method to conduct a team. They settled on a dozen men traveling down the Ohio River, up the Mississippi, and then up the Missouri, which Lewis was to follow until he reached what they hoped was a short stretch of land to the headwaters of the Columbia River and then the Pacific.

Lewis designed a boat with a collapsible iron frame, the building of which took a month to get right. The decision to stay and monitor the progress of the construction of this boat was Lewis' first independent decision, and it cost him precious time. But he was determined to have everything just as he wanted to ensure the expedition's success.

Also, Lewis began to believe that his party needed to be greater than twelve men and was sure he wanted another officer to join the expedition. On June 19, 1803, Lewis wrote to his old friend William Clark and delivered an unusual proposition. Lewis could have asked Clark to be his lieutenant, allowing Clark to retain the overall command. Instead, he asked Clark to be the co-captain of the expedition. Military tradition taught that co-commanders were not typically a good idea. When disagreements arose, there would be no way to settle a dispute between two people of the same rank. But Lewis must have believed there would be no such issue with Clark. They had served and worked together, and they knew the measure of each other. Lewis also selected another officer in case Clark refused, but he would not let this person co-command.

William Clark, at the time, was largely overshadowed by his elder brother, George Rogers Clark, a famed western army commander. They lived in Clarksville, Indiana, after William Clark had left the army due to a medical condition.

Lewis was anxious to hear Clark's reply, and when it finally arrived on July 29, he must have opened it with trepidation. Clark, of course, graciously accepted the offer. Both men agreed that there was no other man in the world they would rather go on this journey with. Lewis asked Clark to begin recruiting acceptable men but warned him that they must be of the best quality; they could not afford lazy, idle, or drunken men on this dangerous campaign. Lewis would pick Clark and his recruits up when he traveled down the Ohio River to Indiana Territory.

Lewis had designed the main keelboat that would be used to travel along the various waterways. It was fifty-five feet long and eight feet wide. He had a mast with two sails, could carry twelve tons, and could be propelled by up to twenty-two oarsmen. As mentioned, the building of this boat resulted in a long delay for Lewis. The builder was a drunk and worked slowly, but he was the only boatbuilder in that part of Pennsylvania. Lewis was forced to constantly beg, plead, and threaten the man to get any work done. To bide his time, he bought a large black Newfoundland dog named Seaman. Finally, on August 31, the boat was completed in the morning. Just a few short hours later, Lewis had loaded the boat and was on his way down the Ohio River.

From the very start, the boat needed to be pushed and pulled much of the way. The Ohio River was especially shallow that season, so Lewis often needed to hire horses and oxen to pull the boat over rapids and low spots. It was exhausting work and made for slow progress. Some days, Lewis and his men only traveled ten miles or less. They would retire, soaked and beaten, only to wake up for another day. Lewis also bought several pirogues, canoe-type boats that could traverse shallow water. These would be loaded while the keelboat was dragged or pushed along.

From the first day on, Lewis made notes in a journal. Lewis and Clark's journals are among the greatest primary texts in American history. They provide a clear chronicle of everything they saw, experienced, and thought about along their epic journey across the continent. However, there are some missing details. For instance, early in the journey down the Ohio River, Lewis dismissed at least three of his men, but we do not know the reason. Lewis does take note of the villages then developing along the Ohio River. These were settlements like Marietta and Cincinnati, where goods were brought to be shipped down the river and then down the Mississippi to New Orleans, where they could be sold in the global market. The men and women of Ohio grew corn and raised hogs and cattle, among other things. Lewis noted that many of the settlements looked well managed; however, he complained that some of the residents were idle and overcharged for services.

Chapter Five: Under Way

While Meriwether Lewis was waiting on his keelboat to be finished, Jefferson received a letter from the governor of Mississippi Territory, William C. C. Claiborne. Jefferson had sent Claiborne a considerable number of questions concerning Louisiana Territory, which he had only learned a few months before was now to be part of the United States. Claiborne tried his best to answer Jefferson's questions, but it proved difficult. Because Louisiana had not been officially handed over, Claiborne did not have access to Spanish documentation concerning the administration of the territory.

Jefferson first wanted to know if there were any reliable maps of the region. Claiborne had none but had heard of the existence of two possibly helpful maps—one by Bernard Romans and the other by George Gauld, the British surveyor of West Florida, whose maps of the Gulf Coast were published in 1803. These maps were practically useless for Lewis and Clark's expedition since the planned path took them northwest of St. Louis. Claiborne also couldn't speculate on the proper boundaries of the territory that the United States had just purchased. The southern portion, containing the Island of New Orleans and the Gulf Coast, was better mapped and more defined. The farther north one went, the less precise the frontier. Claiborne could say that the Spanish colony had been separated into ten divisions: the Island of New Orleans, Point Coupee, Atakapas, Appalousas (Opelousas), Red River, Ouachetas (Ouchitas), Concord, Arkansaws (Arkansas), New Madrid, and Illinois.

Jefferson asked about the Native American population in the territory. Claiborne could say little except that he believed there to be a large, warlike nation, most likely the Osage, along the Arkansas River. Claiborne estimated there were 36,000 whites in the territory and an equal number of slaves. Smuggling, he said, was extremely common. Jefferson wondered about suitable land for growing sugar, and Claiborne could tell the president that there was plenty.

The question about sugar tied in directly with Jefferson's understanding of the expansion of the United States. Americans throughout this period are often called "land-hungry." To better understand this, one can look at plenty of examples. Perhaps the best would be Captain Meriwether Lewis himself. Born in Virginia, Lewis was brought up as part of the land-rich aristocracy that controlled the state. Lewis inherited a large plantation from his father, along with many slaves. As a teenager, he began to manage the plantation called Locust Hill. His primary crop was tobacco, the favorite crop of Virginia planters. Lewis' slaves planted and harvested the tobacco year after year until the soil's nutrients were used up and new fields needed to be plowed. To make a profit, Lewis had to grow huge amounts of tobacco, and because he hardly practiced crop rotation, he needed unimaginable amounts of land. Also, to make profits, the Southern gentleman dabbled in land speculation. So, even after inheriting Locust Hill, Lewis was often on the lookout for other tracts of land. Part of the motivation for going on the expedition in Louisiana was that he was sure to receive land grants for his work.

All in all, it was not unheard of for someone like Lewis, Jefferson, or George Washington to own thousands of acres of land for planting and selling at a profit. The Virginian gentleman was almost always land-rich and cash-poor as a result. The land was bought on credit or with loans. When running a plantation, the threat of bankruptcy was ever-present. This helped to fuel not only the hunger for land but also the reliance on the terrible practice of slavery. It was a system that required a constant supply of new land and therefore a system with an unknown but certain expiration date.

The Northerners were not wrong to be concerned that Louisiana was to be a spreading Virginian empire fueled by Jefferson's Republicanism and the Southern plantation system. However, the Louisiana Purchase transcended even Jefferson's expectations. It was the first clear step towards a United States that spanned the continent and a nation that competed on the global stage. Spain, France, England, and even Russia had a claim to the land west of the Mississippi to the Pacific coast, but it would be America that would own it, eventually.

Lewis and Clark's route.
https://commons.wikimedia.org/wiki/File:Carte_Lewis_and_Clark_Expedition.png

By the time Lewis reached Cincinnati, he knew he would have to spend the winter somewhere near St. Louis. It was too late in the year to begin the journey up the Missouri. He went to Clarksville, Indiana Territory, and finally met up with his co-captain William Clark at the house of Clark's brother, George Rogers Clark. Over the next two weeks, they officially selected the enlisted men for the journey. These would not be the only men to join Lewis and Clark, but they would be the soldiers assigned to what was called the "Corps of Discovery." This unit of the US Army would be the core of the expedition. There was a ceremony for those selected; however, most men who volunteered were not accepted. For the men allowed to join, it was the chance of a lifetime. They would surely experience a great adventure but were also promised land grants upon the expedition's completion.

By now, Lewis had far exceeded the $2,500 that Jefferson had set aside. Lewis was drawing upon War Department funds. He had been permitted to write promissory notes that would be honored by Secretary of War Henry Dearborn. This would be Lewis' method of payment going forward, and he used it extensively. The Corps of Discovery and Clark's slave, York, set off again down the Ohio. They hired a renowned woodsman, George Drouillard, to locate some missing recruits. Lewis was impressed by Drouillard and hired him on to the expedition as an interpreter. By November, they reached the Mississippi and now had to go upstream to St. Louis. They knew that from this moment until they reached the continental divide, they would be traveling upstream and thus against the current. They managed to only travel about one mile per hour. They quickly realized they would need more men to row the oars of the keelboats and canoes.

On November 28, they reached the army outpost of Kaskaskia and were able to raid it for supplies—and about twelve more volunteers. In early December, they reached St. Louis, a bustling settlement with a population of about 1,000. St. Louis was a center for the fur trade and was primarily controlled by French Canadians. The Spanish lieutenant governor, (Carlos) Dehault Delassus, denied Lewis permission to travel up the Missouri until Louisiana had officially been transferred to the United States, an event that would take place in a few weeks. News of the event, of course, would take much longer to get to St. Louis, but Lewis wasn't worried. He knew he would be wintering near the city regardless and had plenty of time before he planned to set out.

Lewis and Clark also arranged for more volunteers. Their party grew to about forty-five. While in St. Louis, Meriwether knew he should be gathering information for President Jefferson. Jefferson did not need to send him a list of questions like he had sent Governor Claiborne about Lower Louisiana; Lewis knew exactly what Jefferson would like to know about Upper Louisiana. The population was about 10,000, including 2,000 slaves. Lewis told Jefferson that many of them were traders and small farmers who could be convinced to move back to the east side of the Mississippi. (Lewis knew Jefferson had begun to imagine creating a vast Native American reservation on the west side of the Mississippi.) However, Lewis warned that there would be difficulties in convincing the slave owners in Upper Louisiana to go into Illinois, which was a free territory. To what extent Lewis or Jefferson believed it would be possible to convince Americans to leave the frontier is unknown; however, at some level, Lewis must have realized it would be practically impossible.

Jefferson was not interested in the possibility of growing sugar in St. Louis, unlike his plans for the eastern side of the Mississippi in Lower Louisiana. The climate prevented it. However, the desire for new land was just as strong there as farther south. This was partly because of the desire for land speculation. Ohio Country had been bought up by land speculators, many of whom had made fortunes. However, a speculator needed to have people buy his land, and in Ohio, this was proving fairly easy. There were scores of people in the eastern states who longed to buy cheap land on which to grow staple crops and raise livestock. It was the earliest form of the American Dream. Native Americans were a threat since this was their land to begin with, but the United States Army was quickly becoming adept at defeating tribes and forcing them to sign treaties that surrendered their land. After the Lewis and Clark Expedition, they only got better. There was still resistance, of course. The confederation of Tecumseh had not yet formed, and the Red Stick War had not yet taken place. Still, even in 1803, Lewis must have realized there was no way to push back the spread of America across the Mississippi River.

Lewis and Clark picked a spot along the Wood River to make their winter camp. Lewis regular visited St. Louis to get supplies and talk to the locals about the coming journey. He obtained a copy of the Mackay map, which showed the Missouri up to the land of the Omaha Native American tribe. Clark also took trips to St. Louis and improved the keelboat, adding multi-purpose lockers and a mounted cannon capable of swiveling 360 degrees. The volunteers received training, including shooting practice, and huts were built to house the volunteers and the captains. During this time, they learned of the presence of the Sioux— who were said to be numerous, well-armed, and hostile—at the mouth of the Missouri.

They continued to train and wait for the winter to pass. Ice floated down the Mississippi as the volunteers grew impatient. Disciplinary measures were required when the volunteers left camp to buy whiskey and get drunk, and fights broke out. At last, the winter passed, and spring began to flourish. Still, Lewis waited. News finally reached the party of the official transfer of Louisiana from Spain to France and then to the United States. Lewis then had permission to finally go up the Missouri, but still he waited.

Governor Claiborne, now officially the head of the government of Louisiana in 1804, was facing his dilemma of whether to act or wait. It was clear that the Anglo-Americans and the white Creoles didn't have much in common, but the one idea that they both supported was white supremacy. A Virginian by birth, Claiborne surely shared in this sentiment, but practicality caused him to act with caution. The New Orleans battalion comprised about 500 free men of color, and they represented the best line of defense for the new territory. Claiborne followed Jefferson's advice and officially recognized the battalion, but this caused the elites of New Orleans to vilify the governor.

White Creoles had opposed the Spanish regulations on slavery and the treatment of free blacks. They hoped that with the Louisiana Purchase and the creation of more republican methods in local government, they could gain control and overturn the Spanish laws. Specifically, they desired to do away with the ability of slaves and others to buy their freedom.

In 1804, free people of color in Louisiana were accustomed to a certain degree of recognition and rights, such as the ability to own lands and slaves of their own, to run businesses, and have access to legal redress. These were things that non-whites in the American South and much of the North did not enjoy. Jefferson himself had made it known that only whites in Louisiana would be given citizenship.

It was assumed by the Jefferson administration that, from among these whites, a large militia could be formed to protect the territory from Native American attacks or invasions by Spain or Britain. But Claiborne was finding this difficult to organize. Whites were spread out on plantations for the most part, and the lack of good roads made it hard to communicate between these plantations. Not just that, but in Louisiana, in 1804, it would be hard to bring together a group of whites who all spoke the same language. Spanish, French, Italian, German, Swedish, English, and American farmers grew sugar and cotton all along the Mississippi above and below New Orleans. If an attack occurred, they would not be able to organize themselves quickly enough or give a command in a single language.

On the other hand, Claiborne recognized that the battalion of color was well organized, well armed, and had a history of successful military campaigns. They were known especially for putting down slave revolts; however, this did not make the whites of Louisiana feel safer. They were angry with Claiborne for officially recognizing them; instead, they had hoped he would disband them and strip free people of color of their rights. Their motivation was primarily grounded in fear. The revolt of Saint-Domingue had rattled slaveholders everywhere. Refugees from the war were just then arriving in New Orleans, and whites in Louisiana feared that what had happened there would happen in their territory.

Claiborne felt stuck in an impossible situation. While he recognized the colored battalion, he also took some advice from Secretary of War Dearborn, who urged him to diminish the battalion, if at all possible, without giving offense. To this end, Claiborne assigned two whites, Michel Fortier and Lewis Kerr, as the battalion's commanders. He instructed them to accept no new members. Hopefully, he reasoned, the issue would be resolved slowly and therefore not be likely to cause the members of the battalion to fight against him. It would also keep the white settlers of Louisiana from starting a riot.

Meanwhile, Meriwether Lewis had finally felt enough time had passed. On May 2, 1804, the party set out from St. Charles and headed up the Missouri River. They were leaving what they considered civilization and expected to be gone for two years. There would be no more communication with Jefferson or Secretary Dearborn. There would be no place to buy supplies. The people they met would be completely unknown to them, mainly Native Americans of tribes they only vaguely knew of, who spoke languages they couldn't begin to comprehend. Before them lay *terra incognita*, almost completely unmapped and uncharted. Their path would take them across the northeastern corner of Louisiana Territory, over the Rocky Mountains, and into a land nominally claimed by both the British and Russians, just north of land belonging to Spain. They had passports to travel into British territory, but they had no guarantee that these passports would be honored if they came across any British. More than that, however, was that the explorers did not have permission from Native Americans to cross their land, and they certainly did not have permission from the wild animals that patrolled the forests. Despite all this, they were happy to get going.

Chapter Six: Struggling Forward

Traveling up the Missouri River proved even more difficult than going up the Mississippi. There were scores of obstacles, including logs or whole trees, sandbars, and whirlpools. Most of the time, the keelboat and two pirogues traveled upriver only by pure manpower. The men used oars when the water was deep enough or poles to push the boats. When all else failed, they got out strong ropes and dragged the boats along. Only occasionally did a beneficial wind arrive and allow the sails to carry them. Still, they made good progress, sometimes as much as twenty miles in a day. The pirogues, one red and one white, were easier to handle. Besides weighing less than the keelboat, they rode much higher in the water. Still, the keelboat was essential for its storing capacity and the protection it afforded them.

During much of the summer of 1804, Clark was on the keelboat, as he was the better boatman and could help drive the men onward. Lewis often walked along the bank or went for long hikes into the surrounding countryside, where he collected specimens and made observations. They made it to Daniel Boone's settlement in May. Boone, the famous frontiersman who blazed the wilderness road into Kentucky, had been granted land in Missouri by the Spanish. Not much is known about Lewis and Clark's visit to the settlement. Did they meet Daniel Boone? Did he give them any advice? We only know they bought a few supplies and then moved on. By June 1, they were at the Osage River.

On June 12, they met a group of fur traders led by Pierre Dorion, Sr., a fifty-five-year-old Frenchman with a Yankton Sioux wife. He could speak Sioux and several other languages, and the party persuaded him to join them as far as Sioux country north of the Platte River. On June 26, they camped near the Kansas River at the site that would one day be Kansas City. Clark weighed the waters of the Kansas and the Missouri and found that the Missouri was heavier, indicating that it carried more sediment. Lewis was busy making observations to determine their longitude and latitude. They found Kansas a beautiful country with plentiful game and many wild bushes with sweet berries. Looking out over large grass prairies with little brooks and small stands of trees, they found it almost overwhelming.

Two days later, their responsibilities reminded them of the nature of their endeavor. Two privates got into a whiskey barrel that one of them was supposed to be protecting and were found hopelessly drunk by a sergeant. A court-martial was called, and the private who tapped the barrel was sentenced to one hundred lashes. The other private was given fifty lashes. Lewis and Clark approved the sentence, and it was carried out. There was no prison on the keelboat, so the privates were released back to their duties afterward. The other volunteers felt the punishment was just. It had been their whiskey rations that the privates had used up so selfishly.

Not much later, a private was discovered asleep at his post, a crime that could carry a death sentence due to the seriousness of the offense. Being on watch meant the chance of fighting back against an attack versus being massacred in your sleep. You held your fellow men's lives in your hands. Luckily for the private, they did not carry out the death penalty. Still, he was given 400 lashes over four days. It might seem harsh, but it was a crucial time in the expedition. On July 21, they reached the Platte River. They were now entering Sioux territory, where the possibility of attack was very real.

Lewis continued to make his observations and collect specimens. One of the volunteers shot and killed a badger, an animal new to Lewis. He dissected it and stuffed it so that it could be sent back to Jefferson. He had already discovered two animals unknown to science: the eastern woodrat and the plains horned toad. He continued to collect plant samples and soil samples and locate spots that might be good for settlements—a clear sign that he was not fully sure of Jefferson's plan to turn this region into a Native American reservation. Clark also made observations, especially concerning the various waterways and how one might navigate them. The Platte River he found to be especially wide but astonishingly shallow. They would continue on the Missouri River.

At around the same time in Lower Louisiana, white residents were composing a message to Congress to express their opposition to the end of the foreign slave trade. They also continued to express to Claiborne their dislike of the status of free people of color in the territory. The governor was somewhat surprised by the white Creoles' reactions. They had lived with these free people of color for decades under Spanish rule, and they represented a large portion of the population, part of the fabric of the territory. However, the white Creoles asked Claiborne to banish any free people of color who might try to speak out for themselves. The governor felt the less said about the situation, the better. He was concerned that harsh punishments would only lead to reprisals and escalate into a race war.

Then, the Spanish government proclaimed that any slave who escaped from Louisiana to their territory of Texas would be granted freedom. Claiborne, who lacked other manpower, began to rely on the colored battalion for protection after the Spanish decree became known in Louisiana. Fear of a slave uprising increased, and Claiborne saw the colored battalion as his best mode of defense if the worst should occur. This did not sit well with white Creoles. As the summer of 1804 wore on, they became increasingly disillusioned with Claiborne's ability to assert the white dominance they felt was needed in Louisiana. They began to consider ways to remove Claiborne from office.

By January 1805, white Creoles and Anglo-Americans were petitioning President Jefferson to remove Claiborne. Claiborne tried his best to defend himself. After the creation of the Orleans Legislative Council, the council disbanded the colored battalion, though they could not legally take their firearms. They established that only white males could serve in the territory's militias. This would be the first step in which the white population of Louisiana began taking away rights from free people of color and excluding them from citizenship. Because this was carried out by the representative government and approved by Jefferson, Claiborne could do nothing about it, regardless of how he may have felt. Louisiana was quickly becoming much more like the rest of the United States despite its considerable cultural differences.

In August of 1804, the Lewis and Clark Expedition continued its journey up the Missouri River, encountering new animals. Lewis killed and examined a bull snake; he killed two least terns and described them in detail in his journal. The men were the first Americans to see a coyote, or "prairie wolf," as Clark called it, but they could not kill it. On August 23, Private Joseph Field killed a buffalo. While the animal was known to science, it was the first time most of the men in the party had seen one. They butchered it and grilled the meat, declaring the tongue the most delicious part.

They had also met their first Native Americans—a group of Oto with a French Canadian trapper who acted as interpreter. They gave the Oto gifts of tobacco, flour, pork, and cornmeal; the Oto gave them watermelons in return. They then met with some lesser chiefs of the Oto. Lewis gave them a speech he had prepared for such occasions. Primarily, it informed them that their old Spanish and French "fathers" were leaving and they had a new father, President Jefferson. Lewis was there to listen to what the Native Americans needed and explained that their new father would provide for them as long as they remained peaceful and traded openly with the Americans. He warned them not to displease their new father.

The Oto listened politely but replied that they needed gunpowder, lead shot, and whiskey. Lewis gave them what he could spare, but it wasn't much. He had brought along gifts for the Native Americans he met with, but the gifts had been planned out and were reserved for the leading chiefs. The Oto head chief, Little Thief, eventually met with Lewis and Clark. Lewis repeated his speech and gave the Oto a few small gifts. The Oto were as unimpressed with the Americans as the Americans were with them. So far, Native American relations were not starting on a promising foot. Still, Little Thief agreed to travel to Washington to meet Jefferson in the spring.

On August 27, 1804, they reached the land of the Yankton Sioux and soon received word that the Yankton would meet with them. Three days later, they met with a group of Yankton warriors, including some chiefs. Both sides were dressed in their full regalia. That night they socialized. Lewis and Clark were able to witness the cultural structure of the tribe. The young and brash warriors were hungry for glory. The old chiefs were solemn and thoughtful. The wives were busily cooking and preparing things for their husbands. The children were lost in play and in awe of the newcomers. The Yankton repeated what the Oto had asked for— gunpowder, lead shot, and whiskey. The captains could give them none. The Yankton let them continue but warned them that the Sioux further up the river might not let them pass.

In September, the party passed open plains filled with herds of bison, elk, and mule deer. They spotted "goats" too spry to be killed or described. In what would become Nebraska, they stumbled upon a prairie dog village. While hard-pressed to catch or kill a specimen, they finally flushed one out of a burrow and gave the first scientific description of the prairie dog, or "barking squirrel." Finally, Clark killed one of the "goats"—a pronghorn. He witnessed the pronghorn running across the open prairie and wondered at their amazing agility and speed—up to sixty miles per hour.

While they were doing exceptionally well at finding and observing the plant and animal life they encountered, they found the human life they met much more difficult to deal with. On September 24, they were in what is now South Dakota and met with three chiefs and many warriors of the Teton Sioux. The interpreters they had could barely communicate with the Native Americans, which helped to aggravate both parties. Lewis gave his standard speech, and the captains handed out medals. They selected one chief to be the primary chief, for reasons unknown, and gave him a cloak and a cocked hat. The chiefs were not impressed. They became belligerent and demanded more presents. Several of the warriors showed signs of hostility. Clark ordered the cannon loaded and the men to take up arms. Lewis was ready to light the cannon as he yelled at the Tetons that he would not be trifled with.

Luckily, one chief, Black Buffalo, called the warriors back. Tensions eased, but things had not gone well. The next day, they visited Black Buffalo's camp, which included at least one hundred teepees. The people there were kind to them, but tensions continued to flare. After a few more close calls, with warriors and soldiers ready to fight, the party could finally move on. They left the Sioux unhappy, having failed to establish a good relationship with the tribe, as Jefferson had hoped for.

On October 20, the party had its first grizzly bear sighting. They were warmly welcomed by the Arikara, a once-great nation severely reduced by smallpox epidemics. Traveling to the Mandan villages farther north, they found the Mandan also friendly. This was good news because they decided to spend the winter near them. There, they established Fort Mandan, with two rows of huts and eighteen-foot-high walls. The Mandan continued to visit them, and they traded. Several men were offered Mandan women for company and took up the offer, though the captains politely refused. Then on November 4, a new visitor arrived: Toussaint Charbonneau, a Frenchman trader and trapper. He had with him two wives, both Shoshone, who had been captured by a Hidatsa raiding party. Lewis and Clark hired Charbonneau and allowed him to bring one of his wives. He chose Sacagawea. She was fifteen years old and six months pregnant.

The captains were not particularly impressed with the Frenchman, but they were excited to have his wife in the party because she knew a little of the Hidatsa language and was Shoshone, a tribe they knew they would meet as they got closer to the mountains. Despite his honest attempts, Lewis was frustrated at how he was getting along in his mission with the Native Americans. He had desired to bring peace between the Arikara and Mandan, shut the Sioux out of any future trade relationship, and ensure peace with the Hidatsa and Blackfeet, but it had all come to naught. He received word that the Arikara had aligned themselves with the Sioux and attacked a group of Mandan. Hostilities were constantly breaking out, and alliances seemed short-lived and not always along tribal lines. The truth was that neither Lewis nor Clark understood the politics of the Great Plains. The only way for young warriors to prove themselves and become leaders was through war, especially raiding another village and killing men, kidnapping women, and stealing horses. Lewis and Clark could no more bring peace to the region than cause the Missouri to flow in the opposite direction, no matter how much they might have wanted it.

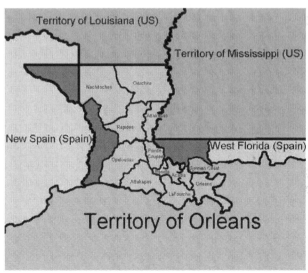

The Territory of Orleans.
Mebigrouxboy, CC BY-SA 4.0 <https://creativecommons.org/licenses/by-sa/4.0>, via Wikimedia Commons; https://commons.wikimedia.org/wiki/File:Map_of_the_Territory_of_Orleans.png

In March 1804, a bill was passed that separated Louisiana into two territories. Effective October, Lower Louisiana, which would roughly become the state of Louisiana, was called the Territory of Orleans. Upper Louisiana, where Lewis and Clark were exploring, would be called the District of Louisiana. Jefferson appointed William Henry Harrison, the governor of Indiana Territory, as the new governor of the district. Harrison quickly went about setting things into order. He split the territory into five districts and advised Jefferson that the militia should be reorganized to allow for plenty of promotion opportunities. (Previously, officers could only become captains.) In October, Harrison took over for Captain Amos Stoddard, whom Lewis had recently dealt with while getting provisions near St. Louis. Harrison had already received a letter from Jefferson making inquiries about the composition of the district and was answering as best he could, just as Claiborne had concerning Louisiana. Harrison was able to give a good account of the population: roughly 8,000 whites and 2,000 slaves.

Another important event in the fall of 1804 was the presidential election, the outcome of which could have had a lasting effect on the Louisiana Purchase. Jefferson was running against the Federalist Charles Cotesworth Pinckney from South Carolina. C.C. Pinckney had been the Federalist pick for vice president under Adams in the 1800 election. Like Jefferson and Lewis, Pinckney was a member of the Southern gallantry. However, he had served under President Adams and firmly believed in a strong federal government. The Pinckneys were a powerful family in South Carolina. Charles' cousin, also named Charles Pinckney, would be governor of the state and strongly supported Jefferson. Jefferson was confident of a victory, but his victory four years earlier showed that a sitting president was not immune to losing an election.

If Pinckney were to win, the administration of the District of Louisiana and the Territory of Orleans might be completely changed. Claiborne's position was at stake, as was Harrison's, while Lewis and Clark might return home to a very cold welcome if the Federalists took control of the government. If any of the expedition party were remotely concerned about it, they did not express those fears in writing. Of course, Jefferson had every right to be confident. He won in a landslide. Jefferson and his running mate George Clinton received 162 electoral college votes, while Pinckney and Rufus King, one of the opponents to the Louisiana Purchase, received only fourteen. Jefferson carried every state except Delaware and Connecticut. Jefferson's previous vice president, Aaron Burr, acted as presiding officer of the Senate and officially announced the victory in February 1805.

Jefferson's accomplishments in his first term, particularly the Louisiana Purchase, were vindicated in his second election. However, his second term would not match his first in success. He had to devise a method to bring Louisiana into the Union without leading to secession and possibly civil war. He had no way of knowing if and when Lewis and Clark might return or their expedition's outcome. It was still to be determined if his investment into Louisiana would pay off. He also still had to determine how to persuade the Native Americans in the southeast to leave their homelands and move across the Mississippi River to completely unknown soil. It would prove more than could be accomplished in just the four years he had left in office.

Chapter Seven: The Edge of the Map

Fort Mandan was located roughly twelve miles from modern-day Washburn, North Dakota. Winters in North Dakota are known to be particularly harsh, and the winter of 1804-1805 was no different. The average temperature hovered around eleven degrees Fahrenheit. Still, the Corps of Discovery had built good shelters, and the fort was strong and the huts warm. The captains rarely stayed in their quarters for very long, however. They were busy through the entire season—meeting with local Native Americans, planning the next part of their journey, and consolidating their records and specimens, which would be sent back down the Missouri along with the keelboat in the spring. It must have been difficult to leave the keelboat, as it had been their home and last mode of defense on many occasions.

On February 11, there was an addition to their party: Sacagawea and Charbonneau's son, Jean-Baptiste. He now supplanted his mother as the youngest member of the party. Clark called the child "Pompey" or sometimes "Pomp." Jean-Baptiste would have no memory of the expedition, but his presence is believed to have benefited the party. In future meetings with Native Americans, Lewis's and Clark's assurances of being peaceful were more readily accepted since no warrior would bring a woman and child to war. The infant would spend the rest of the voyage mostly in a boat or secured to his mother's back.

That winter was hard not only because of the weather but also the constant need for food. The men of the expedition were exerting themselves to their limits and needed to consume around 6,000 calories a day to keep up. Because their meat was from wild game and therefore extremely lean, they could not get the fat they needed to stave off hunger. Their diet was fortified with large amounts of corn from the Mandan and Hidatsa, but the corn was not free. Luckily, Private John Shields was an excellent blacksmith. From scrap, he fashioned a particular type of battle axe the Native Americans had requested. Lewis thought these axes were poorly designed, but he had Shields make them all the same. They could get huge quantities of corn for one axe, and the Native Americans considered it an excellent exchange. The corn was added to the men's diets to keep them from losing the energy needed to drill, patrol, hunt, and stand guard. In other words, without the corn trade, the party might have suffered greatly or completely fallen apart.

Still, they were not completely safe. A group of Sioux attacked a hunting party and got away with two sleighs and two knives, though it could have been much worse. There was only one court-martial during the whole winter when one of the enlisted men hopped over the fort's wall to get in. He was seen by a Native American, who followed suit and gained entry into the fort. The Native American was dressed down, and the enlisted man was sentenced to fifty lashes, but the captains showed leniency and did without the lashes. Otherwise, life in the fort was relatively peaceful and well-ordered. Likewise, the relationships with the Mandan and the Hidatsa were on good terms. The tribes knew a great deal about the lands to the west and were happy to give the information to the captains; in turn, the captains could inform them about life downriver to the Mississippi.

When the expedition had begun, York, Clark's slave, was not completely welcome. The Corps of Discovery was comprised of all white men who knew slavery and viewed African-Americans as less than human. But, by 1805, he was becoming important to the party. He pulled his weight and shared in the trials of the expedition and was fast becoming almost an equal in their eyes. This was not fully recognized by the captains, at least in their journals, but it appears to have happened organically. While he was Clark's "body servant," he could carry a firearm and go on hunting expeditions. He went out as part of a fifteen-man bison hunt in the winter of 1804 and returned with frozen toes, though he luckily didn't lose them to frostbite.

York's presence, like Sacagawea and Pomp, would prove helpful to the party. Native Americans, who had seen only white men before, were usually amazed by York. He was believed to be "big medicine." They marveled at his size (six feet tall and about 200 pounds), athleticism, and dark skin. They often tried to rub the dark shade from his skin, believing it was painted on. Clark encouraged Native Americans to examine York and for York to perform for them. York, for his part, played into the role. He would chase the excited children around the villages, pretending to be a wild animal. The children would scatter before him, giggling in delight. Many Native Americans feared York more than any other member of the party. When the Nez Perce saw him, they called him "Raven's Son." They had considered killing the party but decided against it for fear of retaliation from the "black man." Also like Sacagawea, York would not receive any recognition in his lifetime for his role on the expedition. Even today, very little is known about him.

Lewis and Clark at Three Forks (with Sacagawea and York) by Edgar S Paxson (1912).
https://commons.wikimedia.org/wiki/File:Lewis_and_Clark_at_Three_Forks_by_Edgar_S._Paxson,_1912.jpg

Before they left Fort Mandan, Lewis sent many specimens and notes destined for President Jefferson. Most of the specimens were taxidermy animals and pressings of flowers and plants, along with soil, rock, and water samples. However, he also sent a few living specimens. Most of them died en route, but a living prairie dog and magpie did make it to Jefferson. The president marveled at the animals but did not keep them. He sent both animals, along with other specimens, to Charles Wilson Peale to put into the Peale Museum in Philadelphia.

On April 7, the Lewis and Clark Expedition left Fort Mandan and continued up the Missouri River. They made good progress and found plenty of game along the way, but they also had more encounters with grizzlies. One bear, which they estimated to be about 600 pounds, had to be shot ten times before it died. Bears charged the men and captains on more than one occasion, and the party learned to keep their distance if possible and always keep their guns loaded. As they pressed on, illness became a constant issue. First, Sacagawea became gravely ill; then, Lewis, Clark, and the men had constant complaints. Lewis acted as a doctor as best he could. The summer sun was hot on their backs while the river remained very cold. Mosquitos and prickly pear cactuses were always a problem.

On May 26, Lewis got his first sight of the Rocky Mountains. They were much larger than the Blue Ridge or anything else the men had ever seen. If Lewis or Clark were daunted by the sight of the mountains, they did not relate it in their journals or express it to their men. Everyone was excited to get to—and past—the mountains before winter came. They reached the White Cliffs, the Milk River, and then came to a fork in the river they did not know existed. Their orders were to follow the Missouri to its headwaters, but it was difficult to determine which river was the Missouri. The men all believed that the Missouri went to the north, but the captains became certain it was the south fork. They stuck with the south fork and continued to follow it. Their hunch turned out to be correct.

On June 13, they reached the Great Falls of the Missouri, which today are in Montana and are known as the Five Falls of the Missouri. They had to go around the falls, a seventeen-mile journey on foot. They camped and fashioned two wagons to carry the canoes and supplies. They also brought along the iron-framed boat, which they planned to use as their main vessel along the Missouri. On July 9, they had finally brought everything and everyone around the falls, and the iron-framed boat had been covered with animal skins and sealed. Lewis had wanted to seal it with pine tar, but that had not been available. When the boat was put into the water, the seals broke, and it began to take on water. Lewis had to give up on the boat, which he had spent so much time designing and perfecting. It was buried nearby, but they did not bother to dig it back up on the return journey. Instead, they quickly built more canoes and continued up the river.

On July 27, they reached a place known as Three Forks. This was where Sacagawea had been kidnapped by the Hidatsa, so the Shoshone lived nearby. It was on the western edge of the District of Louisiana, so they knew that the farther they traveled west, the more they entered unclaimed territory and risked encounters with European powers. But this was not their greatest concern. Mainly, they wanted to find the Shoshone and hoped that these Native Americans would be peaceful and willing to trade for horses. These horses would get them over the mountains, or so they hoped. If they could not find the Shoshone or if the Shoshone were not willing to trade for horses, they were not confident that they could cross the Rockies.

They also believed they had reached the headwaters of the Missouri. The three forks were three different rivers. One they named Madison, after Secretary of State James Madison; another they named Gallatin after Secretary of the Treasury Albert Gallatin, and the last they named Jefferson after the president. They decided to follow the Jefferson River and hoped to find the Shoshone somewhere along their path. On August 12, Lewis scouted ahead and came over a ridge where he could see the Continental Divide. All he saw were the Rockies—obviously not one range of mountains, but many. The hope of an easy journey to the headwaters of the Columbia was quickly diminishing.

The next day, Lewis and some men made contact with the Shoshone. For unknown reasons, Lewis had not brought Sacagawea with him, so communication was barely possible through hand gestures. Still, they were lucky. Lewis passed out beads, mirrors, and face paint, which the Shoshone appreciated. They welcomed the party to their village, and Lewis saw with relief that they had many horses. He met Chief Cameahwait, who told them about the "pierced-nosed," or Nez Perce, Native Americans that lived beyond the mountains but traveled through them to hunt buffalo with the Shoshone. This was another good sign since it indicated there must be a way to pass through the mountains nearby. Several Shoshone, including Chief Cameahwait, traveled with Lewis to meet with Clark and the rest of the party. While translating for the captains, Sacagawea recognized Cameahwait as her brother. It was a happy reunion.

The Shoshone agreed to sell them horses and provide a guide, Old Toby (whose real name was Pikee Queenah, or Swooping Eagle), who had traveled through the mountains on the Nez Perce trail. The captains obtained several horses and had saddles built so the horses could carry their supplies. Because they were so far north and at such an elevation, it began snowing as they ventured into the mountains, even though it was only September. They descended into the Bitterroot Valley, where they met the Salish peoples. Here they got a few more horses; they now had thirty-nine, as well as a mule. They then had to cross the Bitterroot Mountains, a particularly hazardous mountain range that led into what is today Idaho. Soon it began to rain, hail, and snow. It was bitterly cold, and the trail was treacherous. There was no game, and they quickly began to run out of food. They resorted to eating some young horses they had with them and candles.

Finally, they came out of the Bitterroot Mountains, fatigued and hungry but all still alive. It would have been impossible without their guide, the Shoshone Old Toby. Clark scouted ahead, hoping to find some food. He instead found a Nez Perce village, and they welcomed him. He met their chief, Twisted Hair, who provided the starving men with dried fish and berries. Lewis and the rest arrived and feasted on the same dried fish and berries, which made them all sick for several weeks. Still, the captains pressed Twisted Hair about what lay ahead of them. They wanted to find the Columbia River and get to the Pacific Ocean before winter set in. Twisted Hair told them they could take a nearby stream, which would eventually feed into the Columbia. They built dugout canoes from ponderosa pines and set out as quickly as possible. It was the first time they had traveled downstream since leaving the Ohio River.

On October 16, they reached the Columbia. They were not completely surprised to find that it consisted of dangerous rapids, often running between massive cliffs. Sometimes they carried their canoes and supplies, but more often, they braved the rapids and survived. They came into the land of the Chinooks, who lived in wooden houses. By October 26, they were in the future Washington state. They kept taking notes, marking down the changing trees that lined the rivers they sped down. They stopped and spoke with the Chinooks, who drove hard bargains, probably because they were used to trading with white men for otter pelts. Lewis found them disagreeable. Clark observed a California condor and believed it must be the largest bird in North America, which it is. Lewis noted the Stellar's jay for the first time and a type of woodpecker that is today called Lewis's woodpecker.

Clark thought he had spotted the ocean on November 7, but he was most likely mistaken. By November 16, however, a member of the party remarked watching the waves break against the shore near the mouth of the Columbia River. They had finally reached the Pacific Ocean, just in time. Winter would be coming soon, and they needed to find a place to settle down. The party voted on the location of their next fort, Fort

Clatsop. (The name came from a group of Native Americans living nearby whom Lewis and Clark believed were called the Clatsop.) Notably, everyone in the party was allowed to vote, including Sacagawea and York. They began construction in early December and completed it on January 1, 1806. It housed thirty-two men, one woman, one baby, and a dog.

Chapter Eight: A Return and Double-cross

James Wilkinson was born in 1757 in Calvert County, Maryland. He was eighteen when the Revolutionary War broke out. He participated in the siege of Boston and became aide-de-camp to Major-General Nathanael Greene. He served under Benedict Arnold and then General Washington, participating in the crossing of the Delaware and the attack on Trenton. He soon became lieutenant colonel and brought the news of the victory of Saratoga to the Continental Congress. He was awarded a brevet promotion to brigadier general. In the process, he leaked information about a conspiracy to replace Washington as commander-in-chief. This almost resulted in a duel with one of the conspirators, but it was dropped, and Wilkinson resigned from the army in 1778.

By 1784, he had moved into Kentucky territory. He promoted an independent Kentucky that should be aligned with the Spanish. At the time, the Spanish charged a hefty toll for any cargo transported down the Mississippi to New Orleans. Wilkinson went to New Orleans to work out a deal whereby Kentucky would not have to pay the toll and would work to benefit Spain. At this time, Wilkinson became a spy for the Spanish and eventually swore an oath to serve the king of Spain. In coded messages, he was referred to as "Agent 13." Wilkinson tried to get Kentucky to split off from the United States and join Spain, but his efforts were unsuccessful. Kentucky soon became the fifteenth state.

In 1791, Wilkinson was called back to duty to fight in the Northwest Territory against Native Americans and possibly the British, who were supplying them. Wilkinson became second in command under General Anthony Wayne, whom he despised. He regularly undermined Wayne's authority. Wayne suspected that Wilkinson was working with the Spanish but died before he could prove anything. With Wayne's death, Wilkinson became the commander of the United States Army. He was still in that position when Jefferson became president and then purchased Louisiana. Wilkinson went with Claiborne to take possession of Louisiana. While he was there, he re-established his ties with the Spanish government. Not long after, Louisiana was split into two territories. In 1805, after William Henry Harrison served as temporary governor of the District of Louisiana, General Wilkinson was named the new governor by Jefferson. Wilkinson was now the governor of the largest territory in the United States and the highest-ranking officer in the army—while still being paid by Spain for information.

Somewhere in all this, Wilkinson was approached by Aaron Burr to be a primary partner in a scheme Burr had developed while still vice president under Jefferson. Burr's conspiracy is not entirely clear and seems to have evolved, but it is clear that Burr believed he could carve out a nation from the western US, Louisiana, Texas, and possibly some of Mexico—of which he would be the leader. He had already approached the British, suggesting that the citizens of Louisiana would prefer to be ruled by England and he could accomplish this if they would provide him with ships and guns. However, England did not respond to Burr's overtures. Burr was undaunted. He believed that, with a small but well-armed force, he could capture all Louisiana territory. With this in mind, he helped convince Jefferson to name Wilkinson to the governorship. By then, Wilkinson and Burr were both committed to the conspiracy.

In April 1805, Burr left the familiar eastern portion of the United States and began his travel west to meet up with Wilkinson and take Louisiana by force. Although his reputation in the east was forever tarnished by his killing of Alexander Hamilton, the people of the west welcomed him as a kind of celebrity. His tour was greeted with fanfare. Women swooned at his piercing blue eyes, and the men secretly laughed at his fancy dress and dandy behavior. Burr then met with Wilkinson at Fort Massac in Illinois, where they stayed for four days. Burr continued to New Orleans. Through the help of rich supporters and his charm, he secured almost a million acres from Spain within the borders of Texas.

Burr would later claim this land was intended to be farmland, but the truth of this was doubted. Burr returned to Washington and continued to work on his plan in secret.

Wilkinson ordered a young officer stationed in Illinois named Zebulon Montgomery Pike to travel up the Mississippi to find its headwaters. Pike left on August 9, 1805. It was the second expedition into Louisiana, but President Jefferson did not order it. Wilkinson only informed Jefferson of the expedition after it had already begun, and Jefferson approved it. Since Lewis and Clark were following the Missouri and then traveling on to the Pacific Ocean, an additional expedition following the Mississippi upstream seemed reasonable. Pike traveled with nineteen men and was gone for eight months and twenty days. This expedition is not often remembered because of Pike's more famous second expedition, but it appears it was something of a test for the young officer. Wilkinson must have already had another expedition in mind after Pike traveled up the Mississippi. Pike's goals were not as scientific as Lewis and Clark's. He was to establish relations with the Native Americans he met and determine the soil quality and possible products from the areas he visited.

While Pike was trying to find the source of the Mississippi, Captains Lewis and Clark and their party were suffering through the winter of 1805-1806. The chief problem was the rain. In their time at Fort Clatsop, they only enjoyed twelve days without rain. They were the first Americans to experience the famous weather patterns of the Pacific Northwest. While they stayed at the fort, the captains worked on their journals and kept the men active. When a whale carcass washed up on a beach near them, they went to investigate and obtain some blubber and oil. But by the time they reached it, the nearby Native Americans had already picked it clean. They settled on bartering for some blubber and oil, which did not last long. Finally, on March 23, they decided to leave the fort and retrace their path back up the Columbia River.

Going up the river was, of course, much harder than going down due to the rapids and the number of falls. They also had to contend with large numbers of Chinookan people near and around them as they traveled. The Native Americans regularly stole from the party, which frustrated Lewis immensely and caused him to lose his patience on more than one occasion. He saw no hypocrisy in this even though he had ordered his men to steal a canoe from the Native Americans when they left Fort Clatsop. Three Chinookan stole Seaman, Lewis' dog, but let the dog go after they were pursued on Lewis' orders.

The going was so slow, and they wanted to be out of Chinookan territory so badly, that they gave up on traveling via the river and burned their canoes. They then marched as directly as possible toward the mountains and the Nez Perce Pass. They stayed for a time with the Wallawalla tribe in late April, from whom they obtained food and horses. They finally reached the Nez Perce and obtained some supplies and horses by setting up a makeshift hospital for the Native Americans to be treated by Captain Clark, who they deemed an excellent doctor. On May 7, 1806, the Bitterroot Mountains came into view. The Nez Perce told them they would need to wait until at least June to cross the mountains because the winter snows had been especially heavy and the pass was blocked by several feet of snow.

The party stayed with the Nez Perce, whom they regarded as a nation of honest people. However, the desire to get over the mountains was hard to resist. Not only would it mean being closer to their homes, but on the west side of the mountains, game was scarce, and they lived mainly on dried fish and roots. They dreamed of returning to the buffalo herds along the Missouri River and knew that, once they crossed the mountains, their path would be almost completely downstream. They hoped to be in St. Louis before the end of the year. Eventually, their impatience got the better of them, and Lewis ordered the men to pack and prepare to cross the mountains. The Nez Perce told them they could not provide any guides, but Lewis decided they would try regardless.

On June 16, they climbed far enough up the mountains to find snow on the ground. Very quickly, the snow was eight-to-ten feet deep. This would have stopped them, but the snow was so compact that it held the weight of the horses, so they pushed on. Without a guide and with the trail completely obscured by the snow, it quickly became impossible to know if they were on the right track. Also due to the snow, the horses had nothing to eat. The captains discussed the situation and decided to return to the Nez Perce. When they got back to the Nez Perce, they hired three guides in exchange for a gun and some horses. By the time they returned to the mountains, the snow had largely melted, and the guides could easily find their way. By June 30, they were descending the mountains and arrived at a spot called Traveler's Rest.

From that point, the party decided to split up. First, Lewis would take nine men and follow the Nez Perce trail to the Great Falls of the Missouri. From there, his party would explore the Marias River in the hopes of meeting some Blackfeet and determining if the Marias went far enough north that the US could claim some of the British territories of Canada. Captain Clark and Sergeant Ordway would take the rest of the men and go to Three Forks. From there, Ordway and ten men would travel down the Jefferson River to the Missouri and then to the spot where the Marias River flows into the Missouri and wait to meet up with Lewis and his men. Clark would go from Three Forks with ten men, Sacagawea, and Pomp. His group would cross the Missouri to get to the Yellowstone River and descend it until it met the Missouri, at which point the party would be reunited.

Meanwhile, back in St. Louis, General Wilkinson was giving another order to his protégé, Zebulon Pike. Pike was to follow the Arkansas River to its source and then travel to the Red River. He would then journey back to the Territory of Orleans or Lower Louisiana. The Red River flows through what is modern-day New Mexico. In 1806, it was very definitely part of Spanish territory. The fact that Wilkinson, a spy for Spain, was sending Pike into Spanish territory does not beg the question of *whether* there were ulterior motives but more *what* Wilkinson's ulterior motives were in sending Pike on his famous expedition. These motives cannot be known for certain, but they likely stemmed from Wilkinson's plans with Burr.

Therefore, it seems possible, if not probable, that Pike was sent into Spanish territory so that he could be captured by the Spanish and gain information on Spanish activities in the southwest and Mexico. However, Wilkinson could also easily claim he had sent Pike into Spanish territory to gather information for the United States, which had an interest in gaining the area that is today Arizona, New Mexico, California, and Texas. Wilkinson's duplicity was well known, so this would fit with his character. It is also possible that by June of 1806, he was beginning to distance himself from Burr. After both the English and Spanish had declined to support Burr, rumors began to spread about his plans to create a new nation in Louisiana and surrounding areas. It was well known that Wilkinson was friendly with Burr, so Wilkinson received word in the summer of 1806 that his name was being tied to Burr and possible treason. He was quickly concerned that his identity as Agent 13 might be discovered, so he was certainly already creating distance between himself and Burr should word reach Washington of Burr's plan.

Whether Zebulon Pike was aware of any of this is unknown. Certainly, he knew he would be entering Spanish territory. Wilkinson instructed him to be discreet and not approach any Spanish settlements. However, it is unclear whether Pike had any idea that this may be connected to the Burr conspiracy, if he even knew about it. Still, his expedition was partly doomed because Spanish spies in St. Louis knew about his journey before his party had even left the city. From Pike's letters to Wilkinson, it is quite clear that he knew he was not only entering Spanish territory but that if the Spanish found him, he might be imprisoned. Still, Lieutenant Pike and twenty soldiers, along with fifty Osage Native American hostages, left Fort Bellefontaine on July 15, 1806. There was one civilian in the party, Dr. Robinson, who was on a mission to Santa Fe to retrieve money owed to a friend of Wilkinson's.

Around this time, the Lewis and Clark party split into five parts. Lewis, the woodsman Drouillard, and Joseph and Reubin Field had made contact with the Blackfeet, but the meeting turned violent when the Native Americans tried to steal the group's rifles and horses. One of the Field brothers had stabbed a Blackfoot in the heart, killing him, while Lewis had shot another warrior in the stomach, which was presumed to be fatal. They had to quickly retreat after the warriors left because they would certainly return with larger numbers and more firepower. Lewis gave up any hope of a peaceful relationship with the Blackfeet and traveled down the Maris River to meet Sergeant Ordway's party as quickly as possible. On July 28, they found Ordway's party. There was no time to waste, so they all got into canoes and let the current of the Missouri take them quickly away.

On August 7, they reached the mouth of the Yellowstone River. They were now out of Blackfeet territory, but instead of meeting up with Captain Clark, they found a note explaining that his party was farther downriver. So, they continued. On August 11, a nearsighted private accidentally shot Lewis in the buttocks, though the soldier denied having shot his captain. The next day, they caught up with Clark, but Lewis was forced to lie face down in a canoe. They finally reached the Mandan and learned that the Arikara and Mandan were at war, the Hidatsa had killed some Shoshone in the Rockies, and the Sioux continued to raid the Mandan, who quarreled with each other. Their hope of peace on the Missouri had completely fallen apart. There was nothing Clark or Lewis could do.

About ten days later, they paid Charbonneau for his services and said goodbye to the Frenchman, his wife, and child. Clark offered to raise Pomp as his son in St. Louis, and Sacagawea replied that she might allow that once Pomp was weaned by the next summer. The party also said goodbye to Private John Colter, who had received permission from the captains to go back up the Missouri River to gather fur. Colter would go on to become the first American mountain man. He would be the first person of European descent to see the region that is today Yellowstone National Park. He was also the first American to describe the Teton Mountains. Then, on September 23, the Lewis and Clark expedition finally returned to St. Louis. By this time, Lewis was fully healed from his wound.

Lewis and Clark had traveled up the Missouri River, crossed the Continental Divide, traveled to the Pacific Ocean, and returned. They had not successfully established a lasting peace among the Native Americans, but they had mapped previously unknown areas. This allowed fur trappers and traders to travel west searching for their fortunes and would eventually pave the way for settlers to arrive on the Great Plains and cross the Rocky Mountains. Lewis discovered 178 new plants and 122 new species of animals. They had collected a vast amount of invaluable information about the Louisiana Territory and its relation to the rest of the continent.

When Lewis and Clark had returned from their expedition, Pike's party was traveling up the Missouri and then the Osage River, where he delivered the hostages that were to be released back to their people unharmed. He parlayed with the Osage and then traveled into Pawnee territory, where they stayed at a Pawnee village. In October, the party split in two. One half was led by Lieutenant Wilkinson, the general's son, and traveled down the Arkansas River and up the Mississippi. They returned to St. Louis without difficulty. Pike's contingent continued west, following the Arkansas River upstream and entering what is today Colorado. There, Pike spotted the mountain named after him, Pikes Peak. In December, he reached Royal Gorge at the base of the Rocky Mountains. However, Pike's group was not prepared for winter in the mountains. They struggled to find the Red River, seemingly lost. Pike pushed south, leaving several men behind who were too fatigued to go on. Finally, they reached a river in southern Colorado that Pike claimed to be the Red River, but it was the Rio Grande. He constructed a fort five miles west of the river.

He was now in Spanish territory, but it is unclear if he realized this. At this time, he let Dr. Robinson continue on his way to Santa Fe. Not long afterward, a Spanish soldier and a Native American found Pike. They informed him that Robinson had arrived in Santa Fe and that Pike's party would be visited by more Spanish. Fifty Spanish soldiers arrived at the fort, leaving Pike no real choice but to surrender when they demanded his party come to Santa Fe.

Pike and his men were now prisoners of Spain. He went from Santa Fe to Mexico, where he met with Governor Salcedo, brother to the last Spanish governor of Louisiana. Since Spain and the United States were not at war, Pike was let go and was able to get some money to bring his men back to St. Louis. The journey allowed Pike to carefully note Spanish forces and the population in Mexico and Texas. Whether this was Wilkinson's plan is debatable. Regardless, by the time Pike had returned, Wilkinson was no longer a supporter of Burr and his conspiracy. In fact, in February of 1807, several months before Pike's return, Burr had been arrested—largely based on information that Wilkinson had provided Jefferson. Wilkinson had told Jefferson that the conspiracy was all Burr's idea and that he himself was still unquestionably loyal. Jefferson was forced to act on the information and had Burr arrested in Alabama. Burr was acquitted of treason and fled to Europe. Wilkinson's treason would not be discovered until long after he was dead.

Chapter Nine: Returning

In 1807, Meriwether Lewis traveled to Washington, D.C., to participate in several events celebrating the expedition. First, he stopped to see his mother at Locust Hill. For his role in the Corps of Discovery, he was awarded 1,600 acres of land. He added this to his other tracts of land in Virginia and Georgia. He was still land-rich and cash poor. In Washington, his accomplishments were praised, and he organized his many specimens for scientists to analyze.

In the winter of that year, Jefferson appointed him governor of the Territory of Louisiana, replacing General Wilkinson. Lewis appeared somewhat uninterested in the job. He remained at home for a year, working on editing his journal for publication, before he traveled to St. Louis to take up the position. He was also trying to recoup expenses from the expedition via the US government. However, the war department refused to pay for things they felt were unneeded, including gifts for Native Americans.

As governor, Lewis settled disputes between Native Americans and Americans, usually siding with the American claims. He prohibited slaves from buying their freedom and barred women from owning land. All the while, he continued to work on his journals. While he had been back east, the territorial secretary, Frederick Bates, had performed his duties. Bates despised Lewis and consistently undermined his authority, writing to President Jefferson to give his opinion on Lewis' inability to do his job.

Bates also wrote to the secretary of war claiming that, instead of trying to get compensation for his out-of-pocket expenses during the expedition, Lewis was trying to profit from them. Lewis found his relationship with Jefferson deteriorating, his financial situation worsening, and he was still unable to publish his journals. If Bates had set out to destroy Lewis, he had succeeded. In 1809, Lewis decided to travel to Washington to defend himself and finally get his journals published. He never made it. On October 11, 1809, Lewis was found with two gunshot wounds in his room at Grinder's Stand on the Natchez Trace in Tennessee. He died shortly after. Jefferson and Clark believed it was suicide, while Lewis' mother claimed he had been murdered. The details of Lewis' death will almost certainly remain a mystery. His passing was certainly a blow to Jefferson, Clark, his family, and the nation that viewed him as a frontier hero.

By that time, James Madison had ascended to the presidency. Napoleon was battling the British and their new ally, the Spanish, in the Peninsular War. Robert Fulton had patented the steamboat. In a log cabin in Kentucky, a child named Abraham Lincoln was born.

Madison would appoint Benjamin Howard as the next governor of the Territory of Louisiana. Under Howard, the territory became smaller and was renamed the Missouri Territory. The Territory of Orleans was still under the leadership of William C.C. Claiborne. The issue concerning the colored battalion had escalated dramatically. In 1807, Claiborne demanded an apology from his nemesis, US Representative Daniel Clark, after Clark had delivered a damning speech concerning Claiborne's supposed preference for the colored battalion. They met in a duel in which Claiborne was shot in the thigh; the bullet lodged in his other leg. He eventually healed and continued his work. Clark was unable to secure his reelection in 1808. Clark did, however, try to expose Wilkinson as a Spanish spy, but he was not believed.

Wilkinson's protégé, Zebulon Pike, returned to St. Louis in 1807. He was not greeted with the same fanfare that Lewis enjoyed. He was not even greeted by his commanding officer because Wilkinson was giving testimony in Burr's conspiracy trial in Richmond, Virginia. In that trial, Judge Timothy Kibby from Upper Louisiana submitted an affidavit that stated that Wilkinson had told him Pike's expedition was not a plan from the government but from Wilkinson, and that if it succeeded, the general would be "placed out of reach of his enemies." It was problematic for Wilkinson, but his testimony against Burr was enough to keep him beyond suspicion. Burr was, however, found not guilty, and Wilkinson returned to his position as commander of the army. In 1809, he appointed Pike the acting military agent of New Orleans. While there, Pike was accused of being part of the Burr conspiracy and a traitor to his country. He bore the accusations in silence.

Pike continued his military career and supported Wilkinson in any way he could. He fought at the Battle of Tippecanoe in 1811 under Gen. William Henry Harrison. When the War of 1812 broke out, Pike was promoted to brigadier general, one of the youngest in the war. He was given the mission to take York in Ontario with 1,600 men. In 1813, he successfully took the city. However, fleeing troops had set fire to many of the buildings in town. One of these buildings contained stores of gunpowder, which exploded and killed several American soldiers, including Zebulon Pike. He was only thirty-four years old. How much he knew of Wilkinson's treason is unclear, though it seems unlikely that Pike would knowingly commit treason himself. Wilkinson was acquitted three times of treason, and it is hard to believe that Pike did not realize his general was duplicitous and self-serving. However, one of Pike's last letters, written just before his march to York, was to Wilkinson. In it, he affirmed his devotion to the general and lamented how Wilkinson had been treated.

Lewis, Clark, and Pike represent the beginnings of a new American archetype: the mountain man. The promise of fur led many into the wilderness. Some simply wanted a chance to farm a plot of land they owned. Eventually, gold, copper, tin, and silver would be found in the mountains and hills of the Louisiana Purchase, and more people would come. Lewis, Clark, and Pike proved that it could be done. It was a risk, of course. Native Americans might kill you—or grizzly bears, rattlesnakes, or outlaws—but if there was even the smallest chance of fortune, plenty of Americans were willing to cross the Mississippi and give it a try.

However, even though the rest of the Louisiana Purchase represented untamed wilderness, the Territory of Orleans was becoming more and more acceptable to the rest of the United States. In 1810, a petition was sent to Washington from the Territory of Orleans requesting admission as a state. This proved to be a rather controversial request when it was read in Congress and sent on to a committee, which had very differing views on the idea of Orleans becoming a state.

One of the primary concerns was that the people of that territory were foreigners, and the US Constitution was meant to apply only to the people of the United States. Some of the representatives did not like the idea of America taking on territories previously held by European powers. They believed the US was acting no different than Napoleon and constructing an empire. Representative Wheaton of Massachusetts wondered just how many states might make up the union if this precedent was set. He asked, "What will become of the old United States?" He and many others were concerned that the center of political power would shift from the original thirteen states to far-flung territories yet to be added. The inclusion of Louisiana as a state was, in their eyes, much different from the creation of Ohio or Kentucky. Those were lands that Americans had settled, pushing out the native inhabitants. The population was derived from the original states, but Louisiana had a large and diverse population from many places besides the United States. In their eyes, it represented a foreign population.

On the other hand, representatives pointed out the commercial and economic importance of the port of New Orleans. It was crucial, they argued, to make New Orleans an equal part of the nation, or there was future danger that they would revolt. The debate continued into 1811.

One of the main sticking points was the inclusion of West Florida in the proposed state. West Florida was originally owned by the British, but the Spanish conquered it in 1781 under Bernando de Gálvez. Then in 1810, American and English settlers declared a portion of the independent Republic of West Florida. This was quickly annexed by the United States, who determined it to be part of the Louisiana Purchase. The proposed state of Louisiana included West Florida. In 1811, a new boundary was drawn to remove much of West Florida from the proposed state; this region would eventually become part of the state of Florida.

The next vote to continue the process, called the Enabling Act, showed the regional division behind the opposition. Almost all of the votes against the bill were from New England. New York, Pennsylvania, and Maryland voted thirty-two for and eleven against. The southern states voted thirty for and five against. The states of the west put all their votes, eight in total, towards continuing the process of giving Louisiana statehood.

Though it was not clearly stated, it is easy to see the influence slavery might have had on these decisions. New England was concerned that Louisiana would represent a first step in a larger expansion of slavery west of the Mississippi. The South, of course, took no issue with this. The middle states were perhaps just as concerned with the economic opportunities in Louisiana as with the spread of slavery. The western states could not very well argue that statehood should not be allowed to go beyond the thirteen original states when they were not part of that original number. Ohio, despite being a free state, put all of its votes toward the Enabling Act.

The act was passed on to the Senate in January 1811 and went to a committee, which more clearly defined the state's boundaries. The Senate committee ensured that only white male citizens had the right to vote. This was a grave concern for the government because it knew that within Louisiana were wealthy people of high status who would not, by them at least, be considered "white." When the bill made it to the Senate floor, there was more opposition. Senator Dana of Connecticut requested that the state only be allowed to enter the union if approved by all of the original thirteen states or by an amendment to the Constitution. This motion was denied by a vote. The Senate finally passed the Enabling Act, and President Madison signed it on February 20, 1811.

Louisiana then called together its constitutional convention to write and ratify a state constitution. This was a long and arduous process that did not conclude until January 1812. The constitution then returned to Congress and was finally signed by President Madison. Louisiana was admitted as a state on April 30th, 1812, exactly nine years after the Louisiana Purchase. In June, the election for governor was held. Though he might have had his detractors, William C.C. Claiborne became the first elected governor of the state of Louisiana.

Before Louisiana became a state, a momentous occurrence took place in January 1812: the steamboat *New Orleans* finished its journey from Pittsburgh to the city of its name. It was the first steamboat to make the trip, but it was far from the last. The venture that proved the viability of steamboats was funded by Robert Fulton and Robert R. Livingston, famed as one of the signers of the Louisiana Purchase.

After his return to the United States, Livingston retired from public life. He turned his focus to developing better methods of agriculture and investing in the development of the steamboat. He was one of the founders of the New York Society for the Promotion of Agriculture, Arts, and Manufactures, published an article about his work raising Spanish merino sheep on his estate (Clermont, in New York), and experimented with different forms of farming. Livingston's brother-in-law was the inventor John Stevens. Along with Stevens, Livingston also worked with Nicholas Roosevelt, who invented paddle wheels for steamboats and was the great-granduncle of President Theodore Roosevelt.

Livingston then partnered with Fulton and developed the first steamboat, *Clermont*, and the *New Orleans*, which was piloted by Nicholas Roosevelt. While Livingston and Fulton enjoyed a monopoly on steamboat traffic along the Ohio and Mississippi Rivers, Livingston often struggled financially. In his lifetime, his role in the Louisiana Purchase was not fully appreciated. However, today most scholars agree that he and Monroe were equally responsible for the positive outcome. Still, Livingston's role as a Founding Father and pivotal part in the expansion of the United States is often overlooked. On February 26, 1813, Livingston passed away at his family home at age sixty-six.

In 1812, the same year he won the gubernatorial elections, William C.C. Claiborne married for the third time. His first and second wives had died of yellow fever while living in New Orleans. His third wife, Suzette Bosque, was the daughter of a Spanish colonial official. Claiborne had firmly established himself as a permanent fixture of Louisiana. It was also in 1812 that the United States declared war on the English for a second time. One of the great concerns of the War of 1812 was an invasion of New Orleans, so Claiborne quickly called together the militia. He also negotiated with the pirate, Jean Lafitte, to help protect the city. Lafitte and Claiborne's militia would join Andrew Jackson's forces and successfully repel a British invasion of New Orleans in 1814. It was a stunning victory even though the war had already officially ended by the time the Battle of New Orleans was fought—the news just hadn't reached New Orleans.

Claiborne's term as governor ended in 1816, but he was then elected to the United States Senate to represent Louisiana. He served from March until November 1817, when he died from what was reported as a "liver ailment." Controversially, Claiborne was buried at St. Louis Cemetery in New Orleans, a Catholic cemetery, even though Claiborne was Protestant. Eventually, his body was moved to Metairie Cemetery. Claiborne Parish is named after him, as is the longest street in New

Orleans. He had a son from his second marriage, William C.C. Claiborne, Jr., and a daughter from his third, Sophronia Claiborne. Claiborne is also the great-great-great-grandfather of the famous fashion designer, Liz Claiborne. Outside of Louisiana, he is unknown, but he undoubtedly played a major role in the territory's transition into the Pelican State.

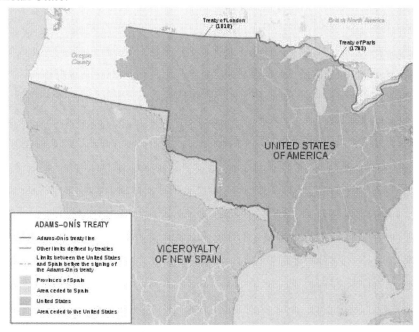

The Adams-Onís Treaty of 1819.

Milenioscuro, CC BY-SA 4.0 <https://creativecommons.org/licenses/by-sa/4.0>, via Wikimedia Commons; https://commons.wikimedia.org/wiki/File:Adams-On%C3%ADs_treaty_map-en.svg

West Florida was left out of the borders of Louisiana as it was still considered a contested region. The War of 1812 showed that there was no longer a threat that England would claim the territory, but by then, Louisiana's borders were already established.

East Florida remained under nominal Spanish rule. However, no one in the US was concerned that Spain would assert its dominance in the region. Spain was having its own difficulties. After the death of Charles III in 1788, the king's son, Charles IV, took control. Charles IV was not as good a ruler as his father. In fact, he left the country's rule mainly to Manuel de Godoy, a royal bodyguard who rose to the rank of prime minister. Godoy gained many titles during his tenure but is best known as the "Prince of Peace." In 1804, Godoy declared war on Britain, which ended in defeat at the Battle of Trafalgar. Godoy allied Spain with France, and this proved disastrous. Napoleon had decided to place his brother, Joseph Bonaparte, on the throne of Spain. Rumors spread that Godoy had sold Spain to Napoleon, and a rebellion arose. Charles IV was forced to abdicate his throne in 1808, and it went to his son, Ferdinand.

Ferdinand did not sit on the throne for a full year before Napoleon had him replaced by Joseph. Napoleon called both Charles IV and Ferdinand to abdicate the throne and end the Bourbon dynasty in Spain. Charles, his wife, and Godoy were kept as prisoners at a royal Chateau and then for three years in Marseilles. In 1813, Napoleon was forced to recognize Ferdinand as the true ruler of Spain. Charles finally settled in Rome at the Plaza Barberini. He apparently had no wish to challenge his son for the throne.

The events of 1808 had begun a shift towards liberalism in the Spanish Empire that would lead to a series of wars for independence in Spanish colonies. The empire was disintegrating, and there was nothing Ferdinand or Charles could do about it. In 1810, Mexico began its war for independence, which would last until 1821. Charles IV, once the ruler of a great empire that included the Louisiana Territory, lived his remaining days in exile. On January 20, 1819, Charles IV died. That same year, Spain and the United States signed the Adams-Onís Treaty, establishing the boundaries between New Spain and the US. In the treaty, Spain gave up any claim to the Northwest and ceded both West and East Florida to the United States. This meant that all the land east of the Mississippi and south of Canada was the property of the United States and that only the US and England had a claim to Oregon Territory. The US assured Spain that they had no interest in Texas.

Chapter Ten: The End of a Beginning

In 1820, Missouri Territory applied for statehood, proposing to allow slavery. This would disrupt the careful balance between free and slave states and threaten to plunge the country into crisis. The House and Senate passed the Missouri Compromise, which allowed Missouri to enter the Union as a slave state while admitting Maine as a free state. In this way, the number of slave states versus free states would remain balanced. The Missouri Compromise also stated that any states formed from the Louisiana Territory above the 36°30' latitude must be free states. This compromise held until 1854 when it was overturned by the Kansas-Nebraska Act. The Supreme Court ruled that the Missouri Compromise was unconstitutional in the *Dredd Scott v. Sandford* decision of 1857. These motions would push the country ever closer to the Civil War, which was rooted in the conflict of slave vs. free states within the Louisiana Purchase.

Missouri became a state in 1821, and President James Monroe—who had been so instrumental in the Louisiana Purchase—signed the Enabling Act that allowed Missouri to create a state constitution. Seeing Missouri become a state must have felt satisfying. Missouri held its first election in 1820, and Alexander McNair defeated William Clark to become the state's first governor. American farmers flooded into the state and established farms along the Missouri River. Native Americans were pushed west, and the original French-speaking population was quickly overwhelmed. It was the first US state fully west of the Mississippi and represented the future of American expansion. In 1817, steamboats began to travel to and from St. Louis. This was the beginning of a robust trade along the Ohio-Mississippi corridor. By 1842, with the completion of the Erie Canal, boats could travel from New York to St. Louis and then to New Orleans without ever traveling on the ocean. By 1850, the population of St. Louis was over 100,000, and Missouri's about 683,000.

In the same year Missouri became a state, Napoleon Bonaparte died on the island prison of St. Helena. The man who had decided to sell Louisiana to the United States had waged war with almost all of Europe and had lost his empire twice. He was just fifty-one years old. Five years later, the man who had made the decision to purchase Louisiana, Thomas Jefferson, died at his home in Monticello. For all the great work Jefferson had done during the American Revolution, as ambassador to France, as secretary of state, and as president, two of his greatest accomplishments were the purchase of Louisiana and the creation of the Lewis and Clark Expedition. His role in the expansion of America and framing the country's future is without question. For good or ill, his policies and opinions helped shape the country for the rest of the century. He died, fittingly, on July 4th, at eighty-three. It was the 50th anniversary of the Declaration of Independence.

Jefferson believed the Louisiana Territory would be well-suited as a place to send Native Americans who would not become "civilized." This idea would finally become a reality in 1830 with the passage of Andrew Jackson's Indian Removal Act. This act established a method by which Native Americans in the southeast could be removed from their homelands to lands west of the Mississippi. The Cherokee, Choctaw, Chickasaw, Muscogee Creek, and Seminole would all be removed, some voluntarily and others by force, to Indian Territory. This was the Trail of Tears, a forced march through horrid conditions in which thousands of Native Americans died of disease, malnutrition, and exhaustion. Whatever Jefferson might have envisioned, the Trail of Tears would be a waking nightmare for Native Americans. The tribes forced to relocate were the so-called "Five Civilized Tribes." These tribes had adopted white culture, dress, and religion and had used slave labor, all in an attempt to become "civilized." According to Jefferson, this should have excluded them from being removed, but they were the main tribes targeted for removal. Indian Territory would eventually become the state of Oklahoma, and the tribes, who were supposed to be left to conduct themselves as they pleased, would be overrun by white settlers and forced to become US citizens.

The frontier of Louisiana was becoming more and more like the rest of America. James Wilkinson, the general, conspirator, and spy, had somehow arranged to become the US envoy to Mexico. He was there when the Mexican War for Independence was finally won in 1821. His former employers, the Spanish, were forced to withdraw from their beloved territory. However, Wilkinson did not go with them. He stayed in Mexico City and requested a land grant in Texas. While awaiting their decision, he died in 1825 at sixty-eight and was buried in Mexico City. In 1854, his identity as Agent 13 finally became public knowledge. Since then, he has largely been vilified by American historians, who see him as nothing more than a traitor. Still, his decision to double-cross Aaron Burr, though undoubtedly self-serving, proved to be the right decision for the United States.

While Wilkinson would later be reviled, James Monroe would be remembered fondly. Monroe had saved the Louisiana Purchase and ensured its successful completion. He had come home as a hero and served as the US minister to England and Spain. He was then secretary of state under Madison and easily won the presidential election after Madison retired. Monroe was the last of the Founding Fathers to be president, and his time in office is often remembered as the "Era of Good Feelings." He presided over the Missouri Compromise and created what would later be called the Monroe Doctrine, which stated that America would resist any European incursion in the Western Hemisphere. After serving two terms, Monroe retired to Oak Hill, his estate in Virginia. After his wife died, Monroe moved in with his daughter and son-in-law in New York City. His health declined, and in 1831 he died on July 4th.

Of the first explorers of the Louisiana Territory, only William Clark still survived into the 1830s. After Captain Lewis died in 1809, the responsibility for editing the journals of their famous expedition fell on Clark. However, Clark felt his writing skills were lacking, so he convinced Nicholas Biddle, president of the Second Bank of the United States, to undertake the daunting task. Biddle and Paul Allen, a historian/editor, completed the work. A biography of Lewis, written by Thomas Jefferson, was published in 1814. It became the standard account of the expedition for the next century. Clark served as governor of Missouri Territory and superintendent of Indian Affairs. He married

Julia Hancock in 1808, and together they had five children. The oldest was named Meriwether Lewis Clark, after Clark's partner and friend. Clark was also the legal guardian of Jean-Baptiste Charbonneau, whom he called Pomp as a baby. After his wife Julia died in 1820, Clark married her cousin Harriet Kennerly Radford. Clark and Harriet had three children. Sadly, she too passed away in 1831.

As the superintendent of Indian Affairs west of the Mississippi, Clark managed the complex relations between the United States and the various Native American tribes in that vast region. He supported Jefferson's view of assimilating Native Americans, but he had to follow President Jackson's removal policy when it became the accepted policy of the country. Clark tried to maintain peaceful relationships, but when he felt it necessary, he would order the use of force. Clark was directly involved in the removal policy of the 1830s and negotiated several treaties that took land away from Native Americans and placed it into the hands of the United States government.

As Clark got older and retired, he moved in with his son, Meriwether Clark in St. Louis. He might have watched the crowds of people, the riverboats, and the general signs of progress and wondered at the changes since he had traveled through the same area with Lewis in 1804. Men, women, and children were traveling up the Missouri River, following the same path he had taken, and were going to farm and live— something that had seemed almost impossible thirty years before. It was no longer an unknown land they went into. Louisiana Territory was constantly shrinking, and states like Missouri, Louisiana, and Arkansas were being formed. The borders were clear, and the land was mapped. It is a mystery what William Clark might have thought as he watched the Louisiana Purchase become more and more a part of the United States. On September 1, 1838, William Clark died at age sixty-eight. His funeral procession was a mile long and was punctuated by the sound of cannons being fired in salute to the great explorer.

Conclusion

The price of the Louisiana Purchase is often given as $15,000,000. It is often regarded as the greatest land deal ever made, and it certainly was. However, a dollar amount does not do justice to the scope of the Louisiana Purchase. For Spain, it represented part of its decline from an empire to a nation. For France, it was not just an influx of desperately-needed cash but the end of the dream of a North American presence. For the United States, it was both a blessing and a curse. Acquiring the land was simply the beginning of a process that would take at least a century. For Native Americans, it was a travesty. It meant that the Americans were coming, and they wouldn't stop until they had control over every square mile of land. It is hard to comprehend just how big the Louisiana Territory was. It included all or part of what would become fifteen states, depending on where you drew the boundaries.

For several generations, it would be *the* American frontier. Jefferson, Livingston, Monroe, and Napoleon were the men who made the deal; Lewis, Clark, and Pike were the men who explored it. Claiborne, Clark, Lewis, and Wilkinson governed it. They were all different forms of frontiersmen, even though Jefferson and Napoleon never set foot in Louisiana. There were many more, of course. Then there were the Nez Perce, Shoshone, Sioux, and Mandan, who showed Lewis and Clark how to survive in this alien land and often saved them from starving. There are the resilient figures of Sacagawea and York, who did so much but received so little recognition in their time. There was General Wilkinson, not a particularly successful spy. Still, even he had his role to play in the creation of the United States west of the Mississippi River.

Had it not been for these people, the story would certainly have been much different. If Napoleon's reconquest of Haiti or Burr's conspiracy had been successful, Louisiana Territory might have looked very different. In the same breath, one should say that the whole world would look completely different, for the fate of that tract of land held the future of the United States. Without the Louisiana Purchase, the world would be a very different place.

Here's another book by Captivating History that you might like

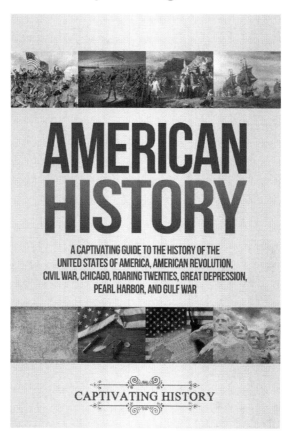

Free Bonus from Captivating History (Available for a Limited time)

Hi History Lovers!

Now you have a chance to join our exclusive history list so you can get your first history ebook for free as well as discounts and a potential to get more history books for free! Simply visit the link below to join.

Captivatinghistory.com/ebook

Also, make sure to follow us on Facebook, Twitter and Youtube by searching for Captivating History.

Works Cited

Louisiana's Admission to the Union (1812),
http://penelope.uchicago.edu/Thayer/E/Gazetteer/Places/America/United_Stat
es/Louisiana/_Texts/LHQ/1/4/Admission_to_the_Union*.html. Accessed 25
February 2023.

James P. "Third Treaty of San Ildefonso." *Mississippi Encyclopedia*, 15 April
2018, https://mississippiencyclopedia.org/entries/san-ildefonso-third-treaty-of/.
Accessed 5 February 2023.

Ambrose, Stephen E. *Undaunted Courage: Meriwether Lewis, Thomas
Jefferson, and the Opening of the American West.* Simon & Schuster, 1996.

Ambrose, Stephen E., and Douglas Brinkley. "The Mississippi and the Making
of a Nation: From the Louisiana Purchase to Today." *National Geographic*,
2002.

"Charles Cotesworth Pinckney." U.S. National Park Service, 17 March 2021,
https://www.nps.gov/people/charles-cotesworth-pinckney.htm. Accessed 18
February 2023.

Claiborne, William CC. "To Thomas Jefferson from William C. C. Claiborne,
24 August 1803." *Founders Online*,
https://founders.archives.gov/documents/Jefferson/01-41-02-0194. Accessed 16
February 2023.

Din, Gilbert C. "Spain's Immigration Policy and the American Penetration."
The Southwestern Historical Quarterly, vol. 76, no. 3, 1973, pp. 255-76.
JSTOR.

"Election of 1804." *Thomas Jefferson's Monticello*,
https://www.monticello.org/research-education/thomas-jefferson-
encyclopedia/election-1804/. Accessed 18 February 2023.

Ermus, Cyndi. "Reduced to Ashes: The Good Friday Fire in Spanish Colonial New Orleans." *Louisiana History: The Journal of the Louisiana Historical Association*, vol. 54, no. 3, 2013, pp. 292-331. *JSTOR*.

Frederick, Julia. "In Defense of Crown and Colony: Luis de Unzaga and Spanish Louisiana." *Louisiana History: The Journal of Louisiana Historical Association*, vol. 49, no. 4, 2008, pp. 389-422. *JSTOR*.

"French Colonial Expansion and Franco-Amerindian Alliances | Virtual Museum of New France." *Canadian Museum of History*, https://www.historymuseum.ca/virtual-museum-of-new-france/colonies-and-empires/colonial-expansion-and-alliances. Accessed 25 January 2023.

"From the Trail to Monticello." *Thomas Jefferson's Monticello*, https://www.monticello.org/thomas-jefferson/louisiana-lewis-clark/framing-the-west-at-monticello/from-the-trail-to-monticello/. Accessed 20 February 2023.

Fulton, Robert, et al. "The Incredible Journey of the Steamboat New Orleans." *Heinz History Center*, 17 October 2017, https://www.heinzhistorycenter.org/blog/western-pennsylvania-history-the-incredible-journey-of-the-steamboat-new-orleans/. Accessed 25 February 2023.

"History of New Orleans | Visit New Orleans." *New Orleans*, https://www.neworleans.com/things-to-do/history/history-of-new-orleans-by-period/. Accessed 25 January 2023.

Hoffman, Paul E. "Luis Unzaga y Amezaga." *64 Parishes*, 4 August 2011, https://64parishes.org/entry/luis-unzaga-y-amezaga. Accessed 2 February 2023.

Hollon, Eugene W. "Zebulon Montgomery Pike and the Wilkinson-Burr Conspiracy." *Proceedings of the American Philosophical Society*, vol. 91, no. 5, 1947, pp. 447-56. *JSTOR*.

"James Wilkinson." *American Battlefield Trust*, https://www.battlefields.org/learn/biographies/james-wilkinson. Accessed 20 February 2023.

Jefferson, Thomas. *Memoirs, Correspondence, and Miscellanies, from the Papers of Thomas Jefferson, Vol. 3*. Edited by Thomas J. Randolph, vol. 3, Project Gutenburg, 2005. 4 vols.

"Jefferson's Instructions to Meriwether Lewis." *Thomas Jefferson's Monticello*, https://www.monticello.org/thomas-jefferson/louisiana-lewis-clark/preparing-for-the-expedition/jefferson-s-instructions-to-lewis/. Accessed 13 February 2023.

Kukla, Jon. *A Wilderness So Immense: The Louisiana Purchase and the Destiny of America*. Knopf Doubleday Publishing Group, 2004.

"Louisiana as a Spanish Colony | Articles and Essays | Louisiana: European Explorations and the Louisiana Purchase | Digital Collections." *Library of Congress*, https://www.loc.gov/collections/louisiana-european-explorations-and-the-louisiana-purchase/articles-and-essays/louisiana-as-a-spanish-colony/.

Accessed 2 February 2023.

"Louisiana Governors 1766-1812." *Louisiana Secretary of State,* https://www.sos.la.gov/HistoricalResources/AboutLouisiana/LouisianaGovernors1766-1812/Pages/default.aspx. Accessed 11 February 2023.

Meany, Andree Chesnel. "La Salle, René-Robert Cavelier, Sieur de." *Encyclopedia of Arkansas,* 19 March 2019, https://encyclopediaofarkansas.net/entries/ren%C3%A9-robert-cavelier-sieur-de-la-salle-2207/. Accessed 25 January 2023.

"Meriwether Lewis - Natchez Trace Parkway (U.S." *National Park Service,* 27 September 2021, https://www.nps.gov/natr/learn/historyculture/meriwether-lewis.htm. Accessed 10 February 2023.

"Missouri Compromise (1820) | National Archives." *National Archives,* 10 May 2022, https://www.archives.gov/milestone-documents/missouri-compromise. Accessed 26 February 2023.

Mizell, Catherine. "Pierre Clément de Laussat." *64 Parishes,* 23 August 2013, https://64parishes.org/entry/pierre-clment-de-laussat. Accessed 12 February 2023.

"National Museum of the United States Army." *National Museum of the United States Army,* https://www.thenmusa.org/biographies/meriwether-lewis/. Accessed 23 February 2023.

Parks, Shoshi. "York Explored the West with Lewis and Clark, But His Freedom Wouldn't Come Until Decades Later." *Smithsonian Magazine,* 8 March 2018, https://www.smithsonianmag.com/history/york-explored-west-lewis-and-clark-his-freedom-wouldnt-come-until-decades-later-180968427/. Accessed 18 February 2023.

Preston, Daniel, et al. "US Presidents / James Monroe." *Miller Center,* https://millercenter.org/president/monroe. Accessed 26 February 2023.

Quintero Saravia, Gonzalo M. *Bernardo de Gálvez: Spanish Hero of the American Revolution.* University of North Carolina Press, 2018.

"Research Guides: Louisiana Purchase: A Legislative Timeline: 1803-1804 (8th Congress, 1st Session)." *Library of Congress Research Guides,* 13 September 2021, https://guides.loc.gov/louisiana-purchase-legislative-timeline/1803-1804. Accessed 11 February 2023.

Rockwell, Sarah. "Pennsylvania Center for the Book." *Pennsylvania Center for the Book,* https://pabook.libraries.psu.edu/literary-cultural-heritage-map-pa/bios/Livingston__Robert. Accessed 25 February 2023.

"Slavery and the Making of America. The Slave Experience: Legal Rights & Gov't | PBS." *Slavery and the Making of America. The Slave Experience: Legal Rights & Gov't | PBS,* https://www.thirteen.org/wnet/slavery/experience/legal/docs2.html. Accessed 13

February 2023.

Staff, NPR, and Andro Linklater. "The Man Who Double-Crossed the Founders." *NPR*, 28 April 2010, https://www.npr.org/2010/04/28/126363998/the-man-who-double-crossed-the-founders. Accessed 5 February 2023.

"Statesman Robert R. Livingston Was Born." *America's Library*, https://www.americaslibrary.gov/jb/colonial/jb_colonial_livingst_1.html. Accessed 5 February 2023.

Sutherland, Claudia. "Haitian Revolution (1791-1804) Global African History" *Blackpast*, 16 July 2007, https://www.blackpast.org/global-african-history/haitian-revolution-1791-1804/. Accessed 7 February 2023.

Wainwright, James E. "William Claiborne and New Orleans' Battalion of Color, 1803-1815." *Louisiana History: The Journal of the Louisiana Historical Association*, vol. 57, no. 1, 2016, pp. 5-44. *JSTOR*.

Williams, Harold D. "Bernardo de Galvez and the Western Patriots." *Revista de Historia de America*, vol. NA, no. 65/66, 1968, pp. 53-70. *JSTOR*.